VIKING SUMMER

The Filming of MGM's 'Alfred The Great' in Galway in 1968

By Mary J. Murphy

ISBN: 978 0 9560749 0 4

Published by Knockma Publishing
Copyright holder Mary J. Murphy © 2008

(Copies of this book available from
morma@eircom.net and from 086 27 67 730)

Printed by JAYCEE

CONTENTS

Dedications vii
Credits ix
Acknowledgements xi
Assistance & Cooperation..xiii
Full List of Cast and Crew of *Alfred The Great* xv
Foreword by Henry Comerford xxi
In the Beginning...xxiii

Chapter One ....*Clive Donner, Bernard Smith, Lord Killanin*........................1
Chapter Two ....*David Hemmings, Michael York, Ian McKellen,*
                      Prunella Ransome, Jim Norton, Sinead Cusack.............19
Chapter Three ....*Film locations, Corrib Crafts, Tom Dowd* 33
Chapter Four ....*Henry Comerford, Christy Dooley, filming at*
                      Castlehackett, UCG student 'extras' 47
Chapter Five ....*Kilchreest, Patrick Stewart, Pat Barrett* 79
Chapter Six ....*The White Horse, John Morris, Canavans*......87
Chapter Seven........*Hugh Harlow, Production Manager on 'ATG'* 101
Chapter Eight ....*Peter Price, Assistant Director on 'ATG'*........................107
Chapter Nine..........*Conclusion* 115

Bibliography..126
About the Author 127

DEDICATIONS

This book is dedicated, with love and appreciation, to my parents Andrew and Bernadette Murphy of Carnmore, formerly of Ballinruane House, Menlough. They fuelled the dreams that eventually led to this work and equipped their four children with the imagination and the determination to see what's around the next bend.

Layers of support are required to cajole a project like this to fruition and in this case that support began and ended with my remarkable husband, Gerard Glynn. He kept the whole show on the road during endless months of domestic disruption, as I dragged everyone in the house along with me on this wild adventure. I thank him for his unwavering encouragement, for filling the last twenty years with love, laughter, wisdom and kindness, and for being the first person to tell me about 'Alfie'.

This book was written, primarily, for our children – Morgan, Mason and Minette – who were fascinated by the unfolding facts of this yarn, and who were spellbound by the glorious diary kept by 12 year-old Sarah Stringer in Galway in 1968.

It's for my sister, Helen, too and her boys Ciaran and Conor, and Martin Carson; for my brother Andy and Cathy and their children Cal and Laurie, and for my brother Seamus and Alison and their children, Ben, Alex and Zara. We include here too the most wonderful of in-laws, Mick and Mary Glynn of Feeragh, and their extended family: Mary Anne and Tony Hoade (Surrey); Martina and Sean Quinn; Cait Cummins and family; Phyllis and Paddy Lee, and Shaun V. Glynn of Saugatuck, Michigan, USA.

Finally, for aunts and uncles Rita Curran, Cepta Corrigan, Al and Betty Murphy, John and Peggy Murphy, Mary and Eamon King and Siobhan Duffy.

CREDITS

CONCEPT AND DESIGN OF BOOK COVER
Senior Graphic Artist Cathy Fleming of 'DeSign Corner', Dublin, who also located our DVD copy of *Alfred The Great*.

Cover photograph – David Hemmings (photographer unknown)

EDITORIAL READERS
Henry Comerford, who set events in an invaluable historical, social and cinematic context.

Angela Burt, whose perceptive feedback, and extreme attention to detail brought rigour and clarity to the manuscript.

David Burke, editor of *The Tuam Herald* newspaper, who brought a lifetime of subediting and technical know-how to bear, along with an avid, consistent and ongoing interest in the subject matter.

All photographs are copyright property of the author unless otherwise stated.

Proofreading by Angela Burt, Portfolio Proofreading Services.

Jack Cunningham, Managing Director, JAYCEE Printers, Galway.
Mary Fahy, Design Supervisor, JAYCEE Printers, Galway.
Damien Goodfellow, Senior Graphic Designer, JAYCEE Printers, Galway.

Particular thanks to Breda Dunleavy of The Arches Hotel, Claregalway, which has served the community since the mid 1800s. Contact info@thearcheshotel.ie or 091 739000

ACKNOWLEDGEMENTS

Amazon

Emer and colleagues in Tuam Library

Maureen Hughes

Laura Bidmead (UK) and Sinead Cusack

Petrina, Galway City Library

Tom Kenny, *Galway Advertiser*

Ronnie O'Gorman; Des Kenny

Gay Byrne

Nanci Young, Smith College, Boston, Mass.

Professor Kevin Rockett, TCD

Dr. Paula Quigley, TCD

The Irish Times

Irish Independent

Irish Press

Evening Press

Daily Mirror

Galway Advertiser

Galway Independent

The Tuam Herald

New York Times

Keith Kelly, *The Connacht Tribune*

Judy Murphy, *The Connacht Tribune*

Sunniva O'Flynn, Irish Film Institute

Orna Roche, Tiernan McBride Library

Marie Mannion, Arts Officer, Galway County Council

Captain Kevin McDonald, Renmore Barracks, Galway

Irish Film Censor's Office

Louise Ryan, Irish Film Board

Ivan Mowse, British Film Institute

Iris Godding, Guild of British Directors (UK)

Charlie Byrne's Bookshop

Elizabeth McLoughlin, Ross Castle

Frances Russell, British Society of Cinematographers

Gearoid Cahill, Computer Consultant

Mrs. Maura Dillon

Sir Ian McKellen

Michael J. Hughes

Jim Carney

Mrs Layne Stringer

IMdB

ASSISTANCE & COOPERATION

With deep appreciation, the author would like to put on record the generous and magnanimous assistance and cooperation of the following:

Robert Molloy, Mayor of Galway in 1968, for the loan of priceless photographs; Henry Comerford, for his marvellous anecdotes, relentless encouragement and gently expressed unwillingness to put up with excess verbiage and digressions in the manuscript; Hugh Harlow (UK), Unit Production Manager on *Alfred The Great*, for his exceptional good humour, extraordinary level of help and background information, and for the copy of his magnificent map-ridden and detail-laden A.L.F.R.E.D. guide, devised by him for senior MGM production staff in the spring of 1968; Peter Price (UK), Assistant Director on *Alfred The Great*, for the loan of his treasured photographs and for allowing us to accompany him as he retraced his steps back to Knockma, when he returned to Galway after a forty year absence in 2008; Christy and Mary Dooley, Galway, for sharing their memories and photographs; Mark Killilea, for telling us about the aerial 'White Horse'; Sarah (Stringer) Whiting, for her astonishing generosity in sharing her exceptionally observant diary, kept while on school holidays in Galway in 1968 with her father, Michael Stringer, Set Designer on *Alfred The Great*. He collaborated on some eight Disney movies and was nominated for an Oscar for his work on *Fiddler on the Roof* in 1971; Tom Dowd of Corrib Crafts, for his vivid descriptions of the feverish activity that ensued following the arrival of MGM to Castlehackett; Gabriel and John Blake, current owners of Corrib Crafts, for their generosity of time and for lending us an envelope-ful of fabulous photographs of Al O'Dea and staff, taken in '68; John Morris of Belclare, for his encyclopaedic knowledge of, and marvellous memories from, filming at Castlehackett; Michael Joe and Sarah Monaghan; Frank Higgins and Leo Courtney, for their time and memories, too; Frank Canavan, Belclare, for telling us exactly where the 'White Horse' was located; Brendan Gannon, Chairman of Caherlistrane Community Parish Council; Paddy, Ina, John, Margaret, Sinead, Cormac and Aisling Hanley; David, Evelyn, Ciara, James, Shannon and Conor Glynn; Michael, Martina, Ronan, Sean and William (Doh) Cunningham; Peadar, Marie-Anne, Seamus, Ciaran, Joanne and Grainne Monaghan - for Ronan Lynch's 'The Kirwans of Castlehackett'; Mr. and Mrs. Willie and Mary Cunningham, Biggera, for sharing their remarkable memories; their son, Dr. John Cunningham, likewise; Kieran and Padraig Reaney, Mossfort, for their immense assistance and support all through the project; Colm O'Dwyer; Fr. Pat O'Brien; Jack Cunningham, JayCee Printers; Mary Fahy, Jaycee Printers; Johnny Morris, son of Lord Killanin; Maurice Burke, Burke's Buses; Conor O'Hagan; Professor Tadhg Foley, Department of English, NUIG; Aidan Walsh; Michael Cooley; Michael 'Chick'

Gillen; Leland Bardwell, poet; Tony Melia (UK); Brendan Forkan; Oliver Muldoon; Nancy Cunningham, Michael Coy; Frank Deacy, for his exuberant descriptions, his posters, and his getting Morgan and me onto the set of *Love and Savagery*, as it was being filmed in Ballyvaughan church in May 2008; Joe Varley, for his detailed recall of night battle filming at Castlehackett; Eamon Nally; Pat Barrett, for his book, MGM receipts and crystal-clear recall; John Mooney and Aidan Mooney; Mr. and Mrs. Patrick Stewart, for their hospitality, for showing us their original sword from *Alfred The Great*, for their Lord Killanin/MGM letter that started the whole ball rolling in October 1967, and for their good-humoured memories; Maura Stewart, for her generous assistance, and Sean Stewart, for copies of the planning permission for the studio complex on their farmland in Eskershanore; Michael Mullery; Joe Callanan, Mrs. Madge Callanan and Mary Callanan Murphy; Ronnie Burke, for his personal set of 19 photographs taken on set as *Alfred The Great* was being filmed at Ross Lake; David Barrett of Edward Holdings; Anne and Ned Waldron; Thomas Hodson; Jack Kinneavey; Sinead Cusack; Sir Ian McKellen, for his carte blanche permission to use whatever we wished from his website; Gerard, Paula and Euan Walsh, for sharing their *Alfred The Great* memorabilia, Peter O'Flaherty of Blueprints Express, Liosban Business Park; Jacinta Fahy; Muiris O'Faoláin, Moycullen N.S.; Michael and Kathleen Reynolds, Ballindiff, for the loan of the 'longship'.

And finally, with much appreciation, the author would like to acknowledge the enthusiasm and encouragement received from the following: Mrs Mary Hernon, Principal of Castlehackett National School, and her wonderful staff; all the children and parents who are lucky enough to enjoy, as we do, the facilities of such an ultra-modern, happy, progressive and safe educational environment; Carrie, Mick, Lisa, Laura and Jack Maloney; Geraldine, Gabriel, Liam, Oisin and Dara Molloy; Padraig, Michelle, Amy and Alan Morris; Ivan, Josephine, Ciaran and Eoin Morris; Séamus, Mary, Christopher, Katie, Lisa and Niall St. John; Tony, Breda, Catherine, Michael, Aine and Molly McHugh; Padraig, Ann, Aoife, Clodagh and Sinead Kilcommins; Denis, Siobhan and Luke Cunningham; Margaret Costello and family (for Maureen Hughes' number, which led on to Sinead Cusack's agent); Sheila Henry; Fionnuala (Mannion) O'Sullivan and family; Anne (O'Brien) English and family; Caitriona (Colleran) Flahive and family and Nuala (O'Donnell) Johnson and family. We mention too Marie O'Halloran, Barbara Clinton and Mary Jane O'Brien, as well as other fellow NIHE Journalism classmates – John Gibbons, Lise Hand, Catherine Moore, Marion McKeone, Aileen O'Meara, Tom Barker, Tara Horan, Conor Lenihan, John Kilrane, Colm Keena, Arminta Wallace, John McGurk and Pam McKay, plus Barbara Chuck and family in Switzerland. Finally, for Marie Mellody (currently also of Switzerland) and family, for her magnificent hospitality in America on numerous occasions. We met on our very first day of school in Ballinruane in 1968, the *Year of Alfred*.

FULL CAST & CREW OF ALFRED THE GREAT

This listing is taken from the July 1969 issue of the movie magazine, *Photoplay*.

Director..Clive Donner
Producer..Bernard Smith
Executive in charge of Production ....Roy Parkinson
Writing credits ....James R. Webb and Ken Taylor

Starring:
David Hemmings ....Alfred
Michael York ....Guthrum
Prunella Ransome ....Aelhswith
Colin Blakely ....Asher
Ian McKellen ....Roger
Peter Vaughan ....Burrud
Alan Dobie ....Ethelred
Julian Glover ....Shrdlu
Vivien Merchant............................Freda
Julian Chagrin................................Ivar
Jim Norton.....................................Thanet
John Rees......................................Cuthbert
Christopher Timothy.....................Cerdic
Peter Blythe...................................Eafa
Sinead Cusack...............................Edith
Barry Evans ....Inglid
Barry Jackson ....Wulfstan
Henry Woolf ....Wenda
Andy Bradford ....Edwin
Keith Buckley ....Hadric
Michael Billington..........................Offa

David Galisyer	Olaf
Eric Brooks	Brother Thomas
Trevor Jones	Sigurd and
Ralph Nossek	Bishop

Original Music	Raymond Leppard
Cinematography	Alex Thomson
Film Editing	Fergus McDonnell
Casting	John Merrick
Production Designer	Michael Stringer
Art Direction	Ernest Archer
Set Decoration	Patrick McLoughlin
Costume Design	Jocelyn Rikards
Hair Stylist	Alice Holmes
Make Up Artist	Tom Smith
Assistant Director	Peter Price
Production Manager	Hugh Harlow
Second Unit Director	Brian Cummins
Sound Editor	Allan Sones
Sound Recordist	Cyril Swern
Special Effects	Robert MacDonald
Paul Stader	Stunt Coordinator
Stunt Double and Archery	Jack Cooper

Other Crew:

Production Associate	Michael Morris (Lord Killanin)
Camera Operator	Tony Spratling
Horse Master	Frederick Ledebur
Gaffer	Frank Wardale

Production companies – Bernard Smith Films, Metro-Goldwyn-Mayer (MGM) (USA) who were also the distributors, and Metro-Goldwyn-Mayer British Studios Ltd (GB). *Alfred The Great* also known as *A King is Born* in the USA.

ALFRED THE GREAT
CREW – FIRST UNIT

Producer, Bernard Smith; director, Clive Donner; production supervisor, Roy Parkinson; production associate, Michael Morris; assistant to production supervisor, Lana Stephens; unit managers, Hugh Harlow, Jack Martin, Ronald Jackson; production secretary, Eileen Matthews; producer's secretary, Pat Pennelegion; 1st assistant director, Peter Price; 2nd assistant director, Brian Cook; 2nd assistant director, Michael Stevenson; continuity, Josephine Knowles; personal assistant to director, Redmond Morris; casting director, John Merrick; director of photography, Alex Thomson; camera operator, Tony Spratling; focus, Harvey Harrison; clapper/loader, Arkadi De Rakoff; sound mixer, Cyril Swern; boom operator, Bill Baldwin; sound camera operator, Ron Matthews; sound maintenance, Peter Martingale; camera maintenance engineer, Norman Godden; production designer, Michael Stringer; art director, Ernie Archer; assistant art director, Norman Dorme; draughtsmen, Alec Gray, Stuart Craig; sketch artists, John Bodimeade, John Rose; set dressers, Patrick McLoughlin, Terry Morgan; property buyers, Denis Maddison, Biddy O'Kelly; scenic artist, Peter Howitt; art department assistant, Ken Court; editor, Fergus McDonnell; 1st assistant editor, Nicholas Napier-Bell; 2nd assistant editor, Christopher Ridsdale; dress designer, Jocelyn Rickards; wardrobe supervisor, Barbara Gillett; wardrobe master, John Briggs; wardrobe assistants, Elvira Angelinetta, Jack Gallagher; chief make-up, Tom Smith; hairdressers, Alice Holmes, Joyce Wood; unit publicist, Julian Senior; chief accountant, Fred Worsley; assistant accountant, Paul Vanderweele; cashier, Cornelius Cremins; accounts secretary, Jean Walter; construction manager, Phil Topliss; construction liaison, Fred Bennett; standby carpenter, W. Mollon; standby stagehand, C. O'Connor; standby rigger, R. Newell; standby painter, A. Smith; standby plasterer, E. Sheppard; standby plasterer's labourer, B. Ellingham; drapes, G. Roberts; grip, Jim Dawes; supervising electrician, Frank Wardale; chargehand electrician, W. Jeffrey.

Electricians, L. Angel, O. Bolter, F. Goodall, G. Greenwood, H. Lazenbury, C. Murphy, J. Smithson, R. Stenterford, E. Turner; electrical maintenance, Peter Tyler; generator operator, R. Warburton; property master, W. Edwards; operating chargehands, S. Hoy, F. Smart, J. Marlow; dressing complex chargehands, B. Smith, W. Beenham; dressing mobile chargehands, H. Colville, J. Palmer; storekeepers, L. Pentecost (Galway base), J. Donaldson, (Kilchreest MGM complex base); property maker, chargehand, A. Thatcher; stunt arranger, Paul Stader; horsemaster, Frank Haydon; chief special effects, Bob MacDonald; special effects, Pat Carr, Jack Redshaw, T. Neighbour; marine department, Michael Turk, John Perry, E. Russell, D. Lenthall; transport manager, Arthur Anderson; Landrover driver, Brian Haskey; Bernard Smith's driver, John Hine; Clive Donner's driver, Gerard Connolly; unit car, Dan Ryan; tractor, Bill McDonagh; generator driver, Ernie Bryan; prop van driver, George Robinson; camera car driver, Ronald Sharp; Cam-El driver, Gareth Meredith; sound truck driver, Jim Hegarty; Chapman Crane driver, Derek Butcher; projectionist, Hugh Cassidy; caterers, Bernard Martin, Frank McGill, Bill Appleby, Les Batson; drivers for artistes and general pickups, Peter Smith, Michael Smith, Ivor Carroll, John Kenney, Peter Geraghty (Oughterard), Frank Duffy (Loughrea), John Duffy (Loughrea), John Gallagher (Gort), John Costello (Galway), William Coffey (Galway), Tom Faherty (Roscahill), Jim Hegarty (Galway), Michael Hanley (Corandulla); assistant unit publicist, Ian Stocks; USA, Bayley Silleck; publicity secretaries, Geraldine Gardiner, Maureen Osborne; stills camera op, Barry Peake; processing, Ken Bray, Clive Sutton.

ALFRED THE GREAT CREW – SECOND UNIT

Director, Brian Cummins; unit manager, Ron Jackson; 1st assistant director, Neill Miller; 2nd assistant director, David Hastings; production assistant, Raymond Becket; continuity, Susanna Merry; lighting cameraman, Jack Atcheler; camera operator, Jim Devis; focus, Keith Jones; clapper/loader, John Golding; grip, Mike Ferris, John Tregar; wardrobe, Ruth Knight; standby carpenter, Pat O'Reilly; standby rigger, Frank Farley; standby stagehand, Ray Saward; standby plasterer, William Brady; standby painter, R. Laws; standby chargehand prop, Roy Cannon; standby prop, P. McDonald; construction van, Joe Egan; electrical van, Tommy Dunn; unit car, Gerry Purcell; props, B. Smith; stagehand, R. Lapper; plant maintenance, Roger Docherty; accountant, Terence O'Connor; special effects, Pat Carr, David Arthur Beavis; assistant to dress designer, Anne Gainsford; electricians, D. Barton, M. Burdett, J. Graham; camera operator, Mike Fox; focus, Tony Coggans. Construction unit: in charge of painters, Wally Cusack; plasterers, A. Baynes; riggers, L. Lawrence; and estimator, L. Burns. Riggers (chargehand) E. Lansbury, B. Anders, L. Chieza, F. Crawford, B. Barrett, T. Lowen, C. Murphy; painters (chargehand) J. Woodward, C. Burke, A. Michael, J. Matthews; wood machinist, M. Scoble; gardeners, J. Gilmartin, A. Gough; plasterers (chargehand) D. Coldham, E. Sheppard, R. Neal, N. Blanchard, D. Sharp, B. Ellingham; plasterer modeller, J. Bourke; chargehand carpenter, J. O'Boy; carpenters, L. Hunt, E. Bailey, M. Fisher, R. Hills; stagehands (chargehand) C. Davies, W. Cannon, P. Hennessey, W. Day, R. Lapper; storeman, Alan Mattocks.

FOREWORD

by Henry Comerford

In October 1967 when *Alfred* arrived in Galway, the city was small, poor and looked a lot like the black and white background to the television series, *Reeling In The Years*. This was pre-Digital, when Renmore was an outlying suburb. I had qualified as a solicitor in 1963 and was only four years in practice with my late father, William Comerford, when Lord Killanin, a friend of my father, called to our office in William Street and informed us that he had recommended us to act as solicitors to Metro-Goldwyn-Mayer British Studios Ltd of Boreham Wood, Hertfordshire, who would shortly be coming to Galway to make a major feature film entitled *Alfred The Great*. Mary Murphy's book, to which these ramblings are intended as a foreword, describes in great and wonderful detail the events that followed that announcement.

Much has been made of the impact of film units on societies in different parts of the world but Galway was so small at the time that you could almost sense the *Alfred* crew invading the city like an army, could feel the presence in the pubs and hotels of the long-haired, pot-smoking – a habit then unheard-of in the West – members of the various branches, the art and props department, the camera operators, set dressers, grips and gaffers, all the strange and exotic species that go to make up a film unit. Many of the construction crew had worked with David Lean in the filming of *Lawrence of Arabia* made only four years before. I saw one of the inscribed watches he presented to all of the members of that crew. These hands-on people drank in O'Connors in Salthill while the more refined individuals, the creative people and the actors, inhabited the Great Southern Hotel in Eyre Square – then the cultural and social omphalos of the city – and the Salthill Hotel.

To place *Alfred* in its filmic context, *Isadora,* the life of Isadora Duncan, directed by the great Karel Reisz, starring Vanessa Redgrave, had just finished shooting somewhere on the Adriatic. Ron Parkinson (Executive in charge of Production on ATG) arrived in Galway to cut the budget of *Alfred*, straight from rendering a similar service to *Isadora.* He was known in the trade for his ruthless budget-cutting techniques as 'the Japanese Admiral'. After his arrival in Galway they used to say jokingly that the battle scenes were cut from 1500 to 15. MGM were, at the same time as the filming of *Alfred*, locked in an epic duel with Stanley Kubrick over the period literally of years that it took to finish his masterpiece, *2001: A Space Odyssey.*

MGM went smash in England over the eventual cost of *2001* and closed down their operations in that country shortly after 1968. '2001' was a huge artistic and commercial success whereas *Alfred*, shooting at the same time, was an unmitigated disaster. Kubrick stayed on in England and never returned to work in America. Carol Reed's *Oliver* won the picture and director's Oscar in 1968 and other outstanding films of that year were *Bullitt*, *The Night of the Living Dead* (first and best version), *Planet of the Apes* (ditto), *The Producers*, *Witchfinder General* and *Carry On Up The Kyber*.

What went wrong with *Alfred*? Mary in her book offers many reasons. I think the concept was doomed from the beginning. The script fell between too many stools; a mixture of swords and sandal made-in-Italy epic and straight historical biography. There was a fatal confusion of styles, and tastes had changed.

The research that went into the writing of this book was formidable. No individual involved and no significant event has been omitted and Mary recreates the extraordinary world of filming and its foibles with style, laconic humour and deadly accuracy. I saw them spraying the dye into the grass when they were doing a retake on the side of Castlehackett Hill, so I can assure you, Mary kids you not.

August 2008

ALFRED THE GREAT ~
IN THE BEGINNING (OCTOBER 1967)

The chucka-chucka din made by Lord Killanin's helicopter blades, as he descended unexpectedly onto Paddy Stewart's farm in Kilchreest in the winter of 1967, imitated precisely the same racket that formed a backing track on the nightly news as Charles Mitchell or Liam Devally announced the daily body count in far-off Vietnam. Killanin swooped from the sky, following an introductory letter sent some time earlier, to request permission of the Stewarts to erect a film studio on their farm at Eskershanore at the foot of the Slieve Aughty mountains between Gort and Loughrea, County Galway. It involved a forthcoming picture, *Alfred The Great*, he explained to his bemused hosts, "which it is hoped to make in Galway".

We can pinpoint the moment with a fair degree of accuracy when Hollywood actually arrived in Galway and sprinkled its magical 'movie dust' around the county because the project received saturation press coverage in the build-up to filming in that long hot summer of 1968. 'Hey, Jude' was the biggest selling pop hit of the year in England and 'Little Arrows' from the Dixies pulled off the same coup in Ireland. Prior to the arrival of the four movie stars, teams of MGM advance personnel had been busy making preparations for months, so when David Hemmings, Michael York, Prunella Ransome and Colin Blakely finally came to make their multi-million dollar 9th century Vikings v Saxons epic, the whole place went wild. That magisterial apparition of cinematic star-power was reported by *The Tuam Herald* of May 11 as having taken place on May 5 (carried in their paper on page 3) under the headline, 'Stars Arrive For Film Epic'.

In the six months leading up to the arrival of Hemmings and Co, scores of MGM personnel and local craftsamen had been hard at work creating a 12,000 square foot purpose-built ultra-modern studio complex on Stewarts' farm. Other preparatory work had been done at Castlehackett, near Tuam (where the spectacular Battle of White Horse Hill would be filmed on a 200ft white horse etched into the side of the hill of Knockma), as well as at Roscahill near Oughterard and at Killinure on the River Shannon. The entire cinematic proposition was a logistical nightmare, likened at the time by Producer Bernard Smith during a conversation with MGM's then legal representative, Henry Comerford, to a real-life battle plan. Hundreds upon hundreds of extras would have to be fed, costumed, transported and accommodated for the duration of a production that was set to run from the winter of 1967 through to the winter of 1968.

Filming was scheduled to begin on 27th May and would continue until September 23rd. Long before the cameras of Oscar-nominated cinematographer Alex Thomson rolled, the director, Clive Donner, Production Designer Michael Stringer and Associate Producer, Lord Killanin, had toured the west of Ireland by helicopter, finally opting for Knockma as the perfect location. The legendary faery hill, reputed burial place of Queen Maeve of Connacht, was then photographed, measured and admired to within an inch of its life, scale models were made and each and every action shot of the battle of White Horse Hill was sketched individually. The details of the making of this extraordinary and sometimes downright astonishing film will unfold in the following pages but to fully appreciate the impact a major cinematic production like that would have had on County Galway at the time, it's vital to try and put things into some sort of social context.

The Ireland of 1968 was a black-and-white place, literally and metaphorically, remaining relatively untouched by the mesmerising events that were unfolding in the wider world. Bobby Kennedy was shot that year, as was Martin Luther King. America was tearing itself apart over the Vietnam debacle, the moon landing was still a year away and the Prague Spring had taken place earlier in the year when Russian tanks invaded Czechoslovakia. This movie invasion of the west of Ireland was an altogether more friendly affair with the ubiquitous appearance of bearded Vikings all over the county during those hot summer months lending a distinct carnival air to proceedings. Locals in all of the affected areas, including denizens of the semi-sophisticated big town that Galway city then was, had never seen anything like it. How on earth could they have done? Certainly, Lord Killanin had been directly involved in the production of John Ford's *The Quiet Man* just past Headford and Ashford Castle in 1951, but there wasn't a vast surge of extras and local craftemen involved in that splendid picture.

Even today, in the post-Celtic Ireland of 2008, the appearance of such a gigantic film production would cause jaws to drop, but when you consider the economic and social circumstances that pertained in rural Ireland in 1968, MGM's arrival must have been nothing short of startling. There was one television channel in Ireland then, one radio station, relatively few cars, an absence of telephones in most homes, mobile phones as yet the stuff

1923 Executions Commemorated

DESPITE bitter cold and a downpour of rain, the annual commemoration of the six Republican soldiers executed at Tuam on April 11th, 1923, was well attended. Led by colour party, guard of honour, Tuam brass and reed band, the C.B.S. boys band, the Presentation girls band and the Galway pipers band, the parade marched from the car park to the old workhouse to the place of execution.

Peadar Hughes (Kilbeg, Headford) said a decade of the Rosary in Irish; Seán O'Gormaile (Tuam) read the Proclamation; Frank Glynn, Co.C. (chairman) read the roll of honour, and Sean MacStiophain (An Uaimh) gave a very fine and stirring oration.

The guard of honour was in charge of Michael Hughes (Kil-

Stars arrive for Film Epic

FOUR of Britain's leading film stars arrived in Galway this week as last minute preparations for the £2½ million epic "Alfred the Great" got under way at the M.G.M. studios near Kilchreest, Loughrea.

David Hemmings, Michael York, Colin Blakley and Prunella Randsom will play the lead roles in the Panavision spectacular which will be shot on location in Co. Galway this summer.

Hundreds of "extras" will be needed for the battle scenes and barbers in Galway are having a lean time as young men allow beards and hair to grow longer in preparation for their film debut.

The objects have been hired for the next six weeks and the M.G.M. buyer estimated their value at over £400.

Knockma, Queen Maeve's fairy hill, is one of the locations which the film unit have selected and workmen are now busily preparing the wooded slopes for the arrival of the camera crews.

Mobile sets are being constructed at the main studio in Kilchreest and will be transported to the different centres as filming progresses. It is believed that from three to five weeks may be spent on the Knockma

Cutting from *Tuam Herald,* announcing arrival of stars in Galway in May 1968.

of science fiction, ditto iPoddy gadgets and digital widgets, no cheap air travel for the masses and priests still saying Mass with their backs turned to their congregations. Back then, too, the country was still in the grip of the damage done to the collective psyche over decades of enforced economic migration when families were wrenched apart with the ease of overcooked chicken limbs.

Then, lo! Into this drab grey place comes the kaleidoscopic madness of Hollywood and its dubious entourage, dispensing excitement and cash in equal measure and involving the participation of hordes of enthusiastic extras from city and county. Army personnel from Renmore Barracks and Defence Force members from further afield are involved, as are hundreds of students from University College Galway, soldiering shoulder to shoulder with secondary school kids who've just "left off", as well as what Bobby Molloy recalled humorously, seemed to have been nearly every taxi driver in Galway. All human life was there and the mad flurry was provided with an extra dash of even more impossible glamour by Hemmings, Ransome and York who flew about the place – separately - in green, white and red open-topped sports cars. David Hemmings, a dashing devil-may-care bounder if ever there was one, went right over the top, as was his wont, by zipping across Galway Bay from his temporary home in Oranmore Castle to Salthill in a high-powered speedboat.

MGM senior people, like Oscar nominee Set Dresser Patrick McLoughlin, were ferried about in boat-sized chauffeur-driven limousines (his being a Rolls-Royce) and the champagne flowed nightly as swiftly as the River Corrib ever did in the social hub of the operation, The Great Southern Hotel in Eyre Square. Marianne Faithfull, Mick Jagger and Christopher Plummer were just some of those who drifted in and out through this miasma of madness and it ran on and on through the full summer. The farmers in the outlying areas who were involved as extras didn't feel in the least bit excluded by the toffs because they were similarly experiencing their own modest orgy of experimentation in the heart of the countryside. The food provided daily by MGM caterers to the crowds of extras and helpers is remembered to this day as having been outstandingly plentiful, arriving in ten-gallon containers – burgers, steak, sausages, spuds, buns and desserts to beat the band. Enough tea and coffee was provided on set daily to refloat the Titanic and every now and then a crate of porter found its way to the thirsty throngs. All that and cash into the hand too. What bliss it was to be alive!

And then suddenly, it's all over. The director shouts "Cut!" for the last time, the cameras fall quiet, lights are extinguished and the whole circus vanishes into the mist like *Brigadoon* as if nothing ever happened. What madness was this? Who on earth was behind this peculiar undertaking? Why was it made? Who chose Galway? How much did it cost? Why did it flop even though millions had been thrown at it? The answers to these and other questions are what we seek to explore in this book and we sincerely hope that you derive half as much enjoyment in reading it as we did in writing it. It's been a long time coming but the research was a thorough-going rocking and rolling blast into the past, with skeletons tumbling from their forty-year old cupboards at a great rate. This is the story of the making of *Alfred The Great* in Galway in 1968, as told four decades later by some of those who were there and who chose to share their memories with us. We thank them and all who made this tremendous adventure back in time possible. Please, enjoy.

Mary J. Murphy, August 2008

ALFRED THE GREAT

starring David Hemmings•Michael York•Prunella Ransome•Colin Blakely
co-starring Ian McKellen.Peter Vaughan.Alan Dobie.Julian Glover and Vivien Merchant as Freda

VIKING SUMMER

CHAPTER ONE

The mystery isn't quite so much how *Alfred The Great* failed as a movie, but rather why on earth anybody ever thought it could succeed? The apparent daftness of it, in hindsight, appears to defy logic. To base a multimillion dollar epic on a fusty-dusty academic book written by a professor of classics who spent her life submerged in the Middle Ages, and then to release it in 1969 at the height of the flower-power era, seemed almost to have invited failure. But we know now that there was more to it than that. This fabulously interesting academic, Eleanor Shipley Duckett, was no arid, unreadable writer and had a huge reputation for appealing to the interests and capabilities of the lay reader. Bernard Smith, the producer of the movie and whose idea it seems to have been to make the film in the first place, came across her book in the course of his own late-night reading. He had a sturdy reputation as a literary editor with Alfred Knopf publishers and was more than competent to tackle seemingly heavy literary matter. Professor Shipley Duckett was indeed a magnificent scribbler with a list of credits to her name as long as a wet week and an excerpt from her *Alfred* book (written for Chicago University Press in 1956) skips and sings and dances off the page. It's no wonder that Bernard Smith was hooked.

Duckett begins her intro by chatting breezily about the ninth century being in all its course the century of Alfred and sweeps along to explain *"We begin our story, then, in the first years of this ninth century: in 802, to be exact, the year in which Egbert, Alfred's grandfather, came on the scene as ruler of Wessex, the kingdom of the west Saxons."*

What Smith must have seen in her book was a fiercely attractive description of the internal conflict permanently bubbling away in the life of Alfred, who was about to become a priest in his 20s when he had instead to don his soldier duds and help fight to save his kingdom. It mirrored the 1960s Vietnam peace v. war quandary of the time crudely but exactly too, and Smith obviously saw parallels that could be transposed into a motion picture.

Cover of Professor Eleanor Shipley Duckett's book, *Alfred The Great* (1956, CUP)

VIKING SUMMER

That push/pull dilemma forms the essence of all addictive drama so when the genesis of MGM's film is looked at through the prism of its own time, it wasn't a madcap notion to make *Alfred The Great* at all. The male lead chosen to play Alfred, David Hemmings, was in his mid-twenties and was at the top of his game, having just starred in Antonioni's *Blow Up* as the snazzy photographer who couldn't separate fantasy from reality. He'd been in *Barbarella* with Jane Fonda just immediately prior to *Alfred* and was one of the three premier counter-cultural iconic male actors in the UK at the time along with Terence Stamp and Michael Caine. Hemmings could easily have been expected to have exuded a suitably spiky, edgy 60s vibe via the persona of Alfred. *Alfred The Great* was dreadfully unsuccessful at the box office and was pummelled unmercifully at the hands of the critics. Of course lots of big movies that should work, don't, and the examples of them are legion. We need only think of Colin Farrell and *Troy* in more recent times, as Michael Coy from Kilchreest, suggested. All we're setting forward here as a modest observation is that the film didn't fail purely because it was an anachronistic ninth century epic. There were lots of other reasons why it didn't make the grade. Critics growled at it and had a go at everything from the dated lingo to the green screen tinge, which apparently resulted from a filter being used on the camera to tone down the glistening sunlight that shone all summer. Ironically, Ireland had actually been chosen because of its famed mist, rain and gloom!

It's a wonder that no one picked up on the speech thing sooner because Ian McKellen tells a story, from the time of filming when he was staying in the old stationhouse in Oughterard, that touches on that awkward use of language. Apparently Harold Pinter was in Ireland visiting his wife on set (Vivien Merchant) and when he heard the lines she had to say he asked Clive Donner (the director, no less) if she could remain mute for that particular scene. McKellen says that Donner agreed to the request, and if that flaw was seen by Pinter at that stage and if Donner acquiesced to his request, the wonder is why they didn't drop all of the "thees and thous" entirely and and modernise the speech.

At a cursory glimpse the epic film could have added up to a perfect ten with perhaps (whisper it) a few Oscar nominations thrown in for good measure. The best of everything was used, starting with the cast and crew. The director, Clive Donner, an accomplished well regarded professional, had already dipped his arms deeply and successfully into the fleshy dough of the movie-making industry. Born in West Hampstead, London on 21 January 1926, his father was a concert violinist and his mother ran a dress shop. Some sources say he began his cinematic career aged 16, some 17 but no matter, he was young. As the grandson of Polish immigrants it's possible that he felt like something of an observer of his host country, hence perhaps adding to his skills of watching and learning. Watching and deciding, for all we know, how he might organise events differently, should he ever get an opportunity to orchestrate things.

After completing his education in Kilburn Grammar School he fetched up one day in Denham Studios where his musician father was at a recording session for *The Life and Death Of Colonel Blimp* (Powell and Pressburger, 1943). He met Michael Powell and began to take seriously the notion of a life in film, thereafter finding gainful employment in the cutting rooms at Denham. He went on to Pinewood Studios after leaving the army in 1947 and undertook an apprenticeship with David Lean - the director who is renowned for gargantuan outdoor epics like *Lawrence of Arabia* and *Ryan's Daughter*. It's that very connection that some said actually led Donner, more than twenty years later, to make his own fantastic rolling narrative, *Alfred The Great*.

Donner wasn't the only participant out of the top drawer on this MGM movie. Talent abounded. Apart from Hemmings, Prunella Ransome was his female counterpart, Sinead Cusack made her cinematic debut in it at the magical age of 19, Jim Norton (best known now for his *Father Ted* appearances) was in there too, as were Ian - now Sir – McKellen, also in his film debut, alongside Michael York, Colin Blakely, Peter Vaughan and Vivien Merchant. American Bernard Smith was the producer and Lord Killanin was on hand as Associate Producer.

The main studios built at Kilchreest near Gort (in south County Galway) were constructed with the intention of enhancing Ireland's place in the world as a location for big budget movies, as Bobby Molloy, then Mayor of Galway, said. The complex was intended to host many more multimillion dollar cinematic projects and was to have replicated the success of Ardmore Studios on the east coast, up and running since 1958, being touted in the newspapers as 'Ireland's New Hollywood'.

A separate Disney film was being made in the west of Ireland in 1968 too *(Guns in The Heather* starring Kurt Russell) and initial plans had been formulated by MGM to make yet another gigantic epic in 1969, based on the Wexford Rising of 1798 and rebel priest, Fr. Murphy. David Lean was to direct it and Robert Bolt - who did the screenplay for *A Man For All Seasons* - was to have written it.

VIKING SUMMER

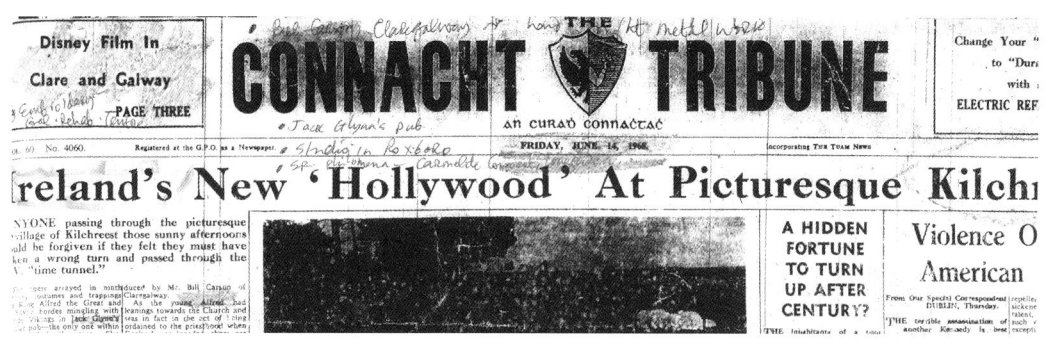

Cutting from *The Connacht Tribune,* heralding 'Ireland's New Hollywood' at the 12,000 square foot purpose-built MGM studio complex at Eskershanore, Kilchreest

In the publicity material used to support *Alfred The Great* and the studio complex, flight times from Shannon to London were given so that potential investors and movie makers would see that it made sound financial sense to base their projects in Kilchreest. It also illustrated that 'rushes' from a day's filming could be sent to London overnight and be back in Ireland again within 24 hours for viewing purposes.

KILCHREEST

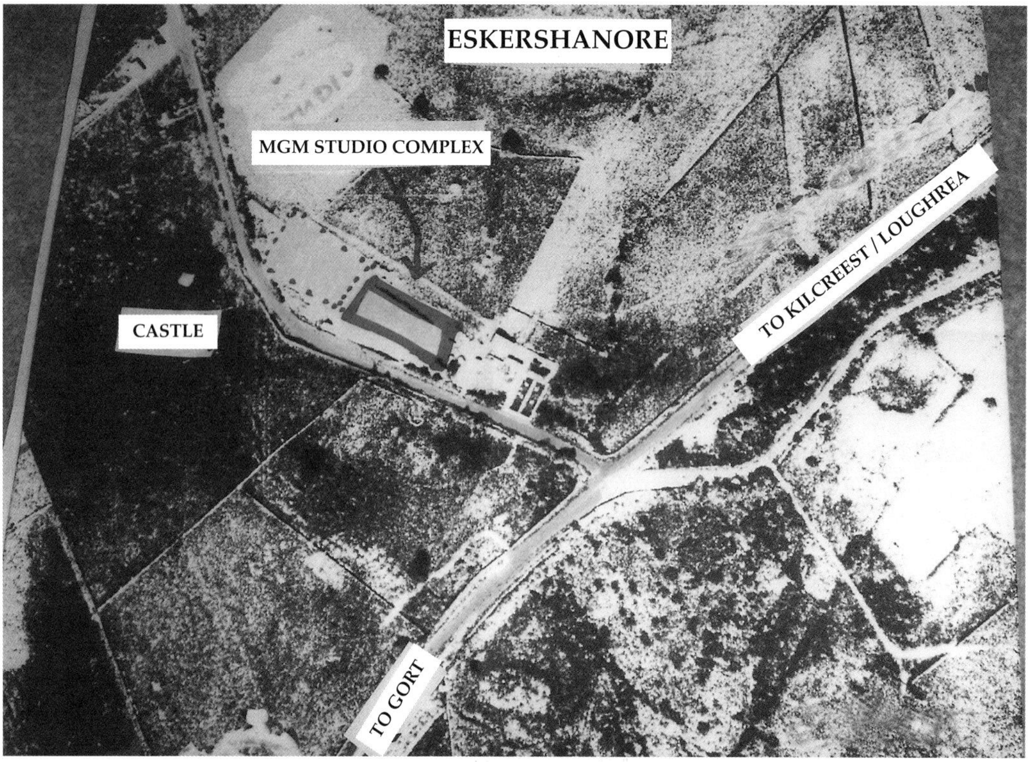

Aerial map of the MGM studio complex in Eskershanore, Kilchreest
(courtesy of Gerard Walsh, current owner of the premises)

Carpenters, craftsmen and artisans worked for months in the lead-up to the production, constructing the main studio building in Kilchreest. Locals in the south Galway town still talk today of the quality of *"the grub"* that was available for all who worked on site. Kilchreest is a small village with just a winding main street, one pub, a shop or two, a lovely well kept church up a hilly side road and that's pretty much it. The studios are out from the village about a mile in the Gort direction (itself home to Lady Gregory's Coole Park and William Butler Yeats' Thoorballylee). The regional *Connacht Tribune* newspaper, a major weekly publication, covered the doings in the village in some style in June 1968. Jack Glynn's pub - the only pub in the village then and now - was the centre of social activity during production, the *Tribune* noted helpfully. From sunrise to sunset the locality was heaving with costumed folks dressed as blond Vikings and Saxon warriors and it reported on June 14 that Bernard Smith, the producer of *Alfred The Great,* was delighted with the progress of the work in hand. He explained to the anonymous reporter that he had devoted four years of his life towards researching the movie, this man who had been an editor before moving into film production in the 1950s to eventually make elaborate multimillion-dollar Oscar-winning films like *How The West Was Won,* shot in magnificent Panavision.

A torrent of facts and figures poured forth from the *Tribune* article, riveting in its precision and showing that everybody's heart was in precisely the right place at all stages during production. Some 30,000 yards of wool cloth, coloured with earth dyes - done by hand and overseen by Costume Designer Jocelyn Rickards - were made to produce the orange and brown colours of the Saxon garb. That colour contrast was done more for cinematic purposes than a strict historical one, in order to distinguish their garb from the harsh blacks and blues of the Viking invaders. Strictly speaking, actual uniforms were a much later development.

Even the very oxen, explained the *Tribune,* that were expertly handled and trained by Joe McNamara to plough and draw the heavy wooden carts from the era, were of the red-horned variety, no traces of modern breeds being allowed to appear in the picture. Their straw harnesses - and 10 miles of it were used - were strictly 'period' and made by Tom Dowd of Tuam's Corrib Crafts. The hand-wrought metalwork varying from the huge cooking pots and urns, right down to the magnificent carved seal of King Alfred, were objects of art produced by Bill Carson of Claregalway. The *Tribune* further explained that as the young Alfred was actually in the process of being ordained when England was invaded, some wonderful church sequences were filmed in a huge 'Cathedral' constructed in the massive Kilchreest studios. Outstanding features were the superb altar cloths and sacred vestments, worked by Sister

VIKING SUMMER

Christy Dooley with an original tapestry (sewn by the Carmellite nuns in Loughrea) and an urn (thrown by Ann Burke, daughter of Harry Clarke) from the movie

Philomena of the Carmelite Convent in Loughrea, which had an international reputation in that craft. Other items worked by the nuns include framed tapestries, like the one now in the possession of Christy Dooley from Galway. His engineering firm in Munster Avenue was responsible for making many of the swords, shields and braziers in the movie. Apparently word had it at the time that real gold threads were used in the making of those tapestries.

The movie storyline was based quite loosely on the work of Professor Shipley Duckett, and can be boiled down to this. At the very time that old England's being ransacked by the roving Danish Vikings, Alfred is on the cusp of being ordained a priest. He grudgingly puts his own wishes to one side and takes up arms against the invaders, leading the English Christians in battle. The Danes are roundly beaten and even though Alfred becomes a hero, he yearns for the priesthood, torn all the while between his passion for God and his lust for blood.

After marrying the beautiful Aelhswith (Prunella Ransome) he gives himself over to his dark

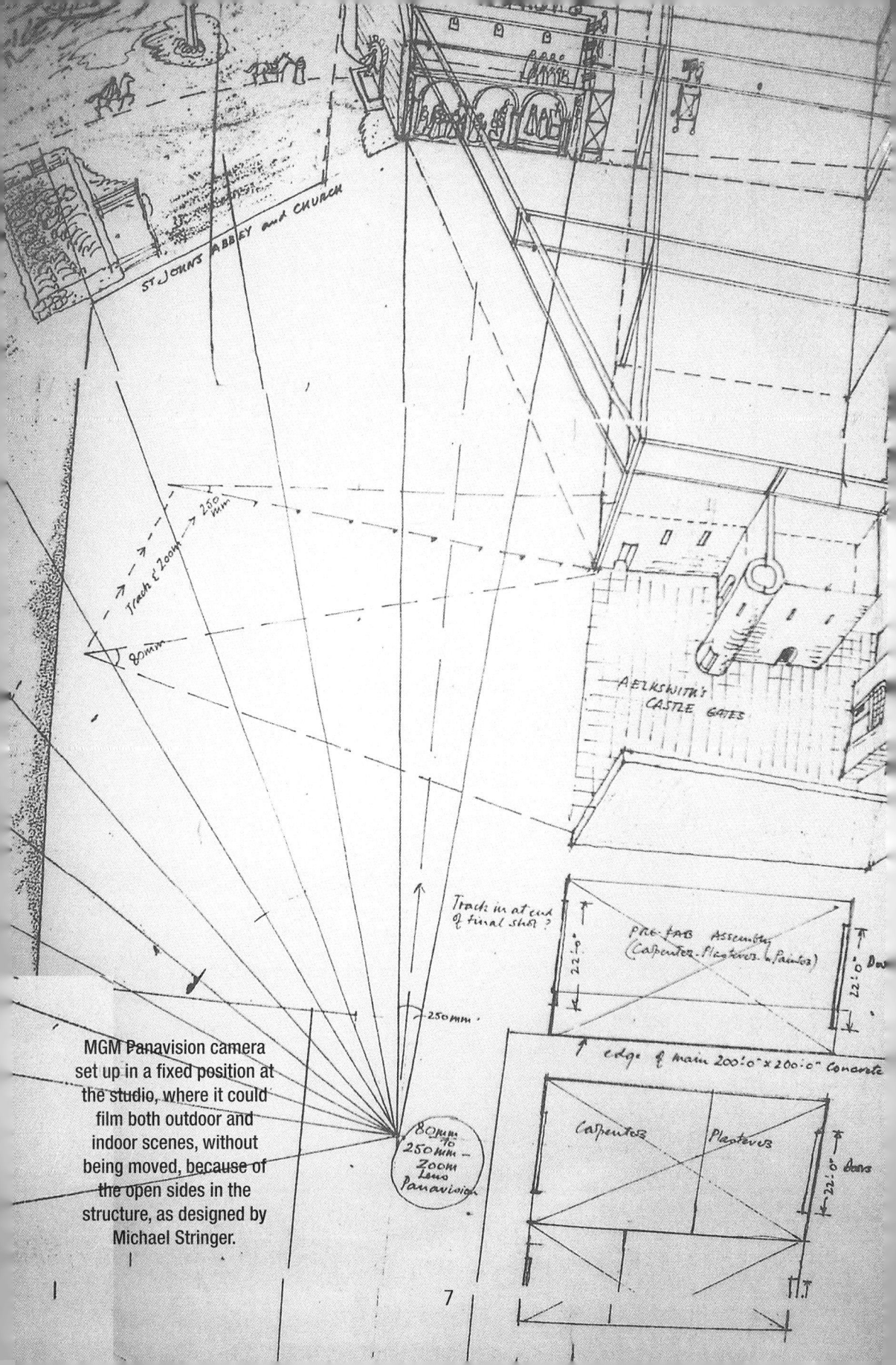

MGM Panavision camera set up in a fixed position at the studio, where it could film both outdoor and indoor scenes, without being moved, because of the open sides in the structure, as designed by Michael Stringer.

VIKING SUMMER

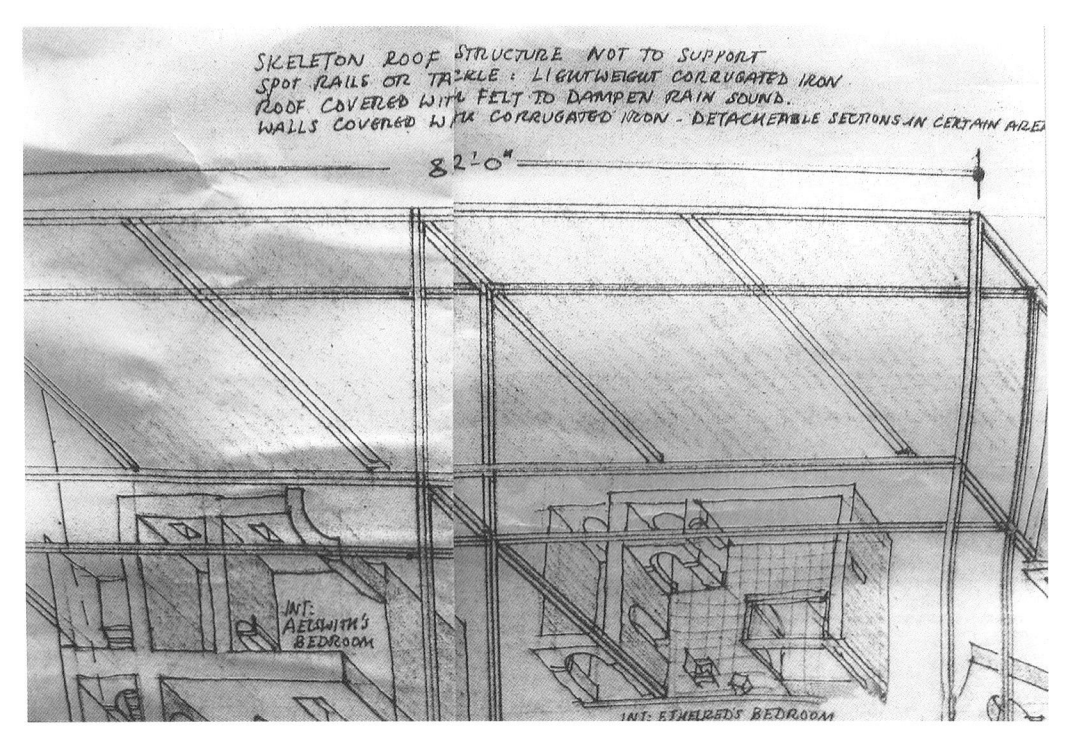

Original drawings of sets in the MGM studio, describing the corrugated felt used to dampen the sound of the rain. Unfortunately it didn't dampen the noise in high winds

side and aggressively and physically assaults his wife. At that point the Danes return and Alfred must muster his English forces one more time for a decisive battle, as well as satisfy the battle raging within his own soul. That's the nub of it, as well as a thread running through of Alfred taking over kingship from his weak elder brother, and it runs to an incredibly long 122 minutes on film. The film was known in America as *A King Is Born* but whatever its title, any movie we see on screen is primarily the result of the vision and the inner thoughts of the director. Clive Donner, the man who drove that vision, in tandem with Bernard Smith, Michael Stringer (Set Designer) and Lord Killanin, opted for the Kilchreest location because of the 360 degree expanse of unspoiled rolling countryside available to them. That vista, which included the slopes of the Slieve Aughty mountains, was enhanced by the design of the studio complex. Michael Stringer constructed it in such a way that the entire front could be opened, allowing the Panavision cameras to be placed in one spot, pointing out towards the elaborate medieval village that had been built beside the studio. The cameras could then follow and track a lengthy unbroken shot from the village outside and swing into the interior sets inside the studio, without moving the camera set-up. The idea was to save both time and money and it was a fantastic plan, based on the old days of filming in Hollywood, as Assistant

Director on *Alfred The Great*, Peter Price, told us. However, like the best laid plans of mice and men it proved to be a mixed blessing.

It worked very well in the vivid sequence where a horseman gallops for unbroken minutes to tell Alfred that the Vikings have arrived, but it fell down on occasion too. That was because the huge corrugated iron sides of the studio structure rattled like demons any time a strong breeze blew, as explained to us by Henry Comerford.

Reports at the time had it that the production in the MGM complex in Kilchreest (an area acceptably known as Fish Ponds, Roxburgh and the townland of Eskershanore as well) cost £12,000 per day to operate, so it was a seriously expensive operation. High hopes were entertained for its success and no one seems to have seen the cinematic train wreck that ensued, coming. Or perhaps, as Henry Comerford, mused, no one cared enough to call a halt. Hundreds of thousands had already been expended in the run-up to the commencement of filming so the juggernaut had to keep on rolling. We've read, too, that the main mover behind the picture, Bernard Smith, expressed himself pleased with the progress of the production and he was the man who involved both Donner and Hemmings, meeting the former in the US just after he'd made a film called *Luv*. Clive Donner was at the height of his considerable powers in 1967/68 having just enjoyed huge success as director of *Here We Go Round The Mulberry Bush*. Smith wanted Hemmings, too, for the lead role, because he was sizzling hot at the time. He'd been in The *Charge Of The Light Brigade* in 1967 (as was Prunella Ransome) and went on to reach spectacular heights of popularity a year later in Antonioni's *Blow-Up*. That film captured much of the *zeitgeist* of the 1960s and was said to have been based on the career of the photographer, David Bailey, played by Hemmings as Thomas.

The arrival of Donner and his stars had been announced in early May 1968 prior to filming beginning on May 27th. The filming moved from Kilchreest to Roscahill to Killinure to Castlehackett, with two main production units (under the management of Hugh Harlow and Jack

Bernadette and Andrew Murphy in The Warwick Hotel, Galway, 1960

VIKING SUMMER

Replica of the White Horse used in the film, drawn by Morgan Glynn (age 9)

Martin) covering requirements. It's hard to imagine that such excitement took place in a building that has since lain abandoned for years in between playing host to a boat-making company (Tullycraft Marine) and a tan-and-hide facility. Most recently the MGM studio has been bought by Gerard Walsh, who generously shared his *Alfred The Great* memorabilia for this project, but in those sun-filled glory days of the summer of 68, it was a thriving hub of bustling cinematic excitement.

As a family we've had our own tangential connection with the film because our father, Andrew Murphy, once owned a red white-faced horse in Ballinruane House which had belonged to the man who trained all of the animals in the picture - Joe McNamara – and the lineage of that horse went all the way back to an appearance in the film.

The stars were accommodated in only the finest quarters (Hemmings got Oranmore Castle, Michael York was put up in Creganna Castle, Ms Ransome was billeted in Lough Cutra Castle and Ian McKellen (then at the foothills of his now stellar career), stayed in an architecturally restored apartment in Oughterard.

The film brought a serious boom to many of Galway's small indigenous industries which were called on to provide furnishings and fittings for the mock-up village. Corrib Crafts from Tuam, said *The Tuam Herald* of May 11, made scores of thrones, benches and timber furniture for the castle. George McGrath, also of Tuam, provided wrought ironwork and Dooley's iron

Michael Stringer and family – wife Ann, daughter Charlotte and son, David

foundry in Galway made shields, armour and goblets for the production. The Tuam antiquarian, D. J. Murphy, lent almost fifty pieces from his collection to the MGM team and that bag of swag included the likes of candlesticks, several items of straw-work and rushwork, wooden dishes and ladles, paint and corn grinders, spades, pans, fishing nets, brooms, spear and axe heads.

Mobile sets were constructed in Kilchreest and transported to Knockma where it was estimated that filming would take between three and five weeks on the side of the 552 foot-high-hill. Some 450-500 soldiers participated as extras during the battle of White Horse Hill shot there at Castlehackett and they received special training at the headquarters of the Western Command in Mellowes Barracks under the command of Colonel P.J. Kearns. Amazingly enough, some of the older men who participated in the movie – from the 1st Infantry Battalion – had been stationed out near Castlehackett in 1939 during what is

VIKING SUMMER

quaintly called 'The Emergency'. We also read that members of the British Olympic Fencing team trained the soldiers in swordsmanship skills.

Those men who weren't trained in Renmore were put through their paces as oarsmen on the river Shannon and were taught how to propel the Viking ships.

While all of that was going on in Galway, more work was underway about fifteen miles north of the city at Castlehackett, where we find Knockma. There, a half-mile-long road was dug and laid up the side of the hill and one of the biggest Viking camps was built on location there. People who live in Kilconly and beyond have said that they could see the collection of tented huts quite clearly from their homes. At the same time Corrib Crafts in Tuam (run by Al O'Dea) was making some eighty ornately carved nine-foot tent poles. Then of course there was the magnificent 200-foot-long outline of the white horse (replicating the original one in Berkshire) that had to be etched out of the side of Knockma in order to form a backdrop for Alfred's Battle of White Horse Hill.

It was Clive Donner's excellent track record that enabled him to realise his long standing ambition to direct on a large scale but *"the expensive flop"* which was *Alfred The Great* may have cast a shadow which lingered around his name for some years after its release. We didn't come across his name again in connection with a movie until *Vampira* from 1974. Mr. Donner turned 82 in January 2008.

He was married to Jocelyn Rickards (RIP), the Australian-born artist and costume designer

A letter addressed to Michael Stringer, while he was staying in The Salthill Hotel

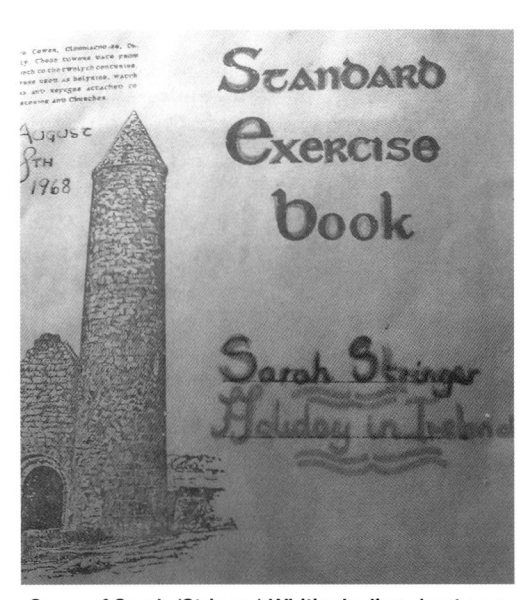

Cover of Sarah (Stringer) Whiting's diary, kept as a 12-year-old schoolgirl while on holiday in Galway during the filming of *Alfred The Great* in 1968

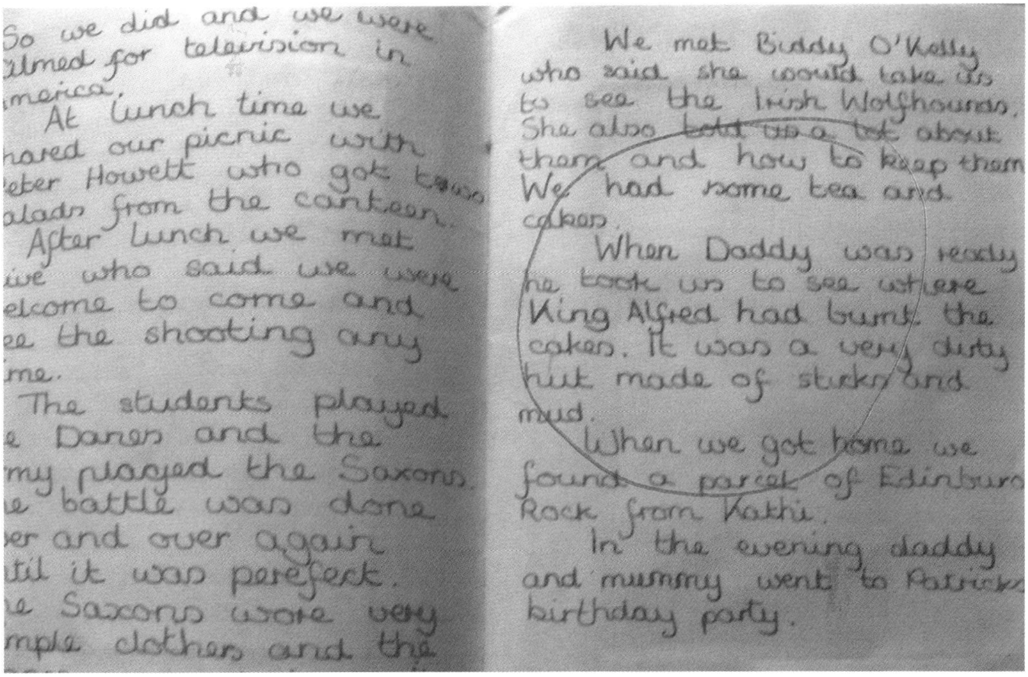
So we did and we were
ilmed for television in
merica.
At lunch time we
hared our picnic with
eter Howett who got two
alads from the canteen.
After lunch we met
ive who said we were
elcome to come and
ee the shooting any
me.
The students played
e Danes and the
my played the Saxons.
e battle was done
er and over again
til it was perefect.
e Saxons wore very
mple clothes and the

We met Biddy O'Kelly
who said she would take us
to see the Irish Wolfhounds.
She also told us a lot about
them and how to keep them.
We had some tea and
cakes.
When Daddy was ready
he took us to see where
King Alfred had burnt the
cakes. It was a very dirty
hut made of sticks and
mud.
When we got home we
found a parcel of Edinburg
Rock from Kathi.
In the evening daddy
and mummy went to Patricks
birthday party.

Extract from Sarah (Stringer) Whiting's Diary

who gave many British movies of the 1960s their distinctive 'look' and they actually met on the set of *Alfred.* It was reported that she was frequently exasperated during her time spent on the movie by some Irish extras who stripped off their scratchy costumes in the intense summer heat and flung them into the nearest bushes! Her last major film was David Lean's *Ryan's Daughter.*

In the March 1969 issue of the British movie industry trade magazine, *Photoplay,* there's a fine interview done during the making of the movie between writer Julian Senior and the director, in which Donner explains how film locations were chosen in Galway. (Julian Senior was also publicist for the movie while it was being made.) *"The choice of this location for the Battle was a crucial one. We felt that we couldn't improve on fact and because certain 9th century historians had carefully described the area where Alfred defeated Guthrum and the Danes, we had to find a location to match the historical record. We needed a gently sloping hillside down which the Danes would march and which was bordered on both sides by woods in which the Saxon ambush parties would wait. Castle Hackett here in County Galway fitted the bill on every count."* Donner said in *Photoplay* that the white horse was "an extraordinary visual aid." Over the months some ten tons of gorse and bushes were cleared off the site, the ground levelled, grass sown, and the outline dug (by hand) to a depth

VIKING SUMMER

Set drawing of 'St. John's Abbey', located in the MGM complex, Kilchreest

of some two feet. It was then filled with twenty-five tons of white plaster laid on to a chicken-wire frame. So dramatic did the horse look from the air that Donner decided *"to film from our recce helicopter during the final stages of the actual battle, to give a bird's eye view of the conflict".*

Donner was apprehensive on the morning of the filming of the battle and told Junior that he wasn't sure why. *"Everything that could possibly have been done to make this a successful screen battle has been done... If it turns out to be a run-of-the-mill blood and blunder affair, then I shall feel we've not succeeded."*

The film was received poorly on its release in July 1969 and almost every aspect of it, except the amazing battle scenes, was heavily criticised. When we saw the film for first time on New Year's Eve 2007 (a copy of which was located for us by Cathy Fleming of deSign Corner), the visceral power of the Danish chanting during the Battle of White Horse Hill, and their inexorable approach into the jaws of the Saxon trap in the valley, were fantastic. Perhaps an extra frisson of excitement was present because it was filmed on the hill that we see out the window daily, one which we've climbed uncountable times over the last twenty years, but it's an exceptional piece of cinematic choreography nevertheless.

THE FILMING OF MGM's 'ALFRED THE GREAT' IN GALWAY IN 1968

Sarah Stringer's photo of the inside of the MGM studio, taken in 1968. Note all of the trunks, cases, paraphernalia and props of the film company

Photograph of the inside of the same building in 2008. Note the presence of skins, pelts and hides.
(© Mary J. Murphy)

As Donner made his way to the hill, the work on the sets and props had been completed long since. Tom Dowd of Corrib Crafts in Tuam was responsible for the making of much of the timber and wooden articles for the sets (benches, bedsteads, thrones) and he explained that he was working away one day when Michael Stringer arrived, unannounced, into their converted Protestant National School. (Gabriel and John Blake, from Manchester, are now running Corrib Crafts). Little did Tom know then that Stringer had worked on eight Disney movies and was to go on to be nominated for an Oscar for his work on *Fiddler on the Roof* in 1971.

Michael Killanin

METRO-GOLDWYN-MAYER BRITISH STUDIOS LTD.

"ALFRED THE GREAT"   M.G.M. 105
                          17th May 1968

UNIT LIST   SECOND UNIT

GRADE	NAME	ADDRESS & TEL. NO:
DIRECTOR	BRIAN CUMMINS	

Lord Killanin's signature on the Unit Lists from 17 May 1968. Courtesy of Bill Stamm

VIKING SUMMER

As Production Designer on *Alfred The Great*, Stringer was responsible for the coordination and design of the sets. In the 1950s he'd worked on things like *An Alligator Named Daisy (1955)* and *Windom's Way*, and when he died in 2004 an obituary in *The* (London) *Independent* said that he had always been in love with films, even as a teenager. A man who paid extreme attention to detail, as Tom Dowd will attest, he was acknowledged by his peers as an immense design talent. His daughter, Sarah Stringer Whiting, was kind enough to lend us her original diary from August 68 which she kept as a 12-year-old schoolchild while on holiday in Galway during the filming of *Alfred The Great*, and its contents are mesmerisingly observant, concise and oozing with description. Born in Singapore in 1924, Michael Stringer enjoyed especially happy memories of his months spent in Ireland, as did Sarah, and always spoke warmly of that time and of the people he met there.

Norman Dorme, who joined Stringer on many movies (including *Alfred The Great*) explained that Michael had a distinctive way of working, marking him apart as a Set Designer of unique distinction.

"Michael did storyboard sketches but he also did an aerial view of the set. All of his sketches were like that. No one else I worked with ever did that sort of thing. It gave a tremendous amount of information. They were very precise and detailed."

Stuart Craig worked on *Casino Royale* with Stringer and recalled the work he'd underaken on *Alfred The Great* in that long hot summer of 1968.

"Michael did amazing and complicated and splendid designs in rural Galway. We built a temporary studio on some farmland and dressing rooms and a generator. And I remember we had the opening shot rather like the Bayeux Tapestry in that you saw this horseman galloping past peasants in wheatfields growing flax and building haystacks and mending carts, and the landscape was designed and dedicated to this particular shot."

Craig elaborated: *"The big sound stage that we built (in Kilchreest) had an open side so that the horseman was able to ride through this rural landscape up to the door of a chapel and then dismount and walk into the chapel which was built inside the stage so you got this most amazing long-developing shot. It was very very ambitious and a sign of his bravery. That's the kind of thing Michael was capable of."*

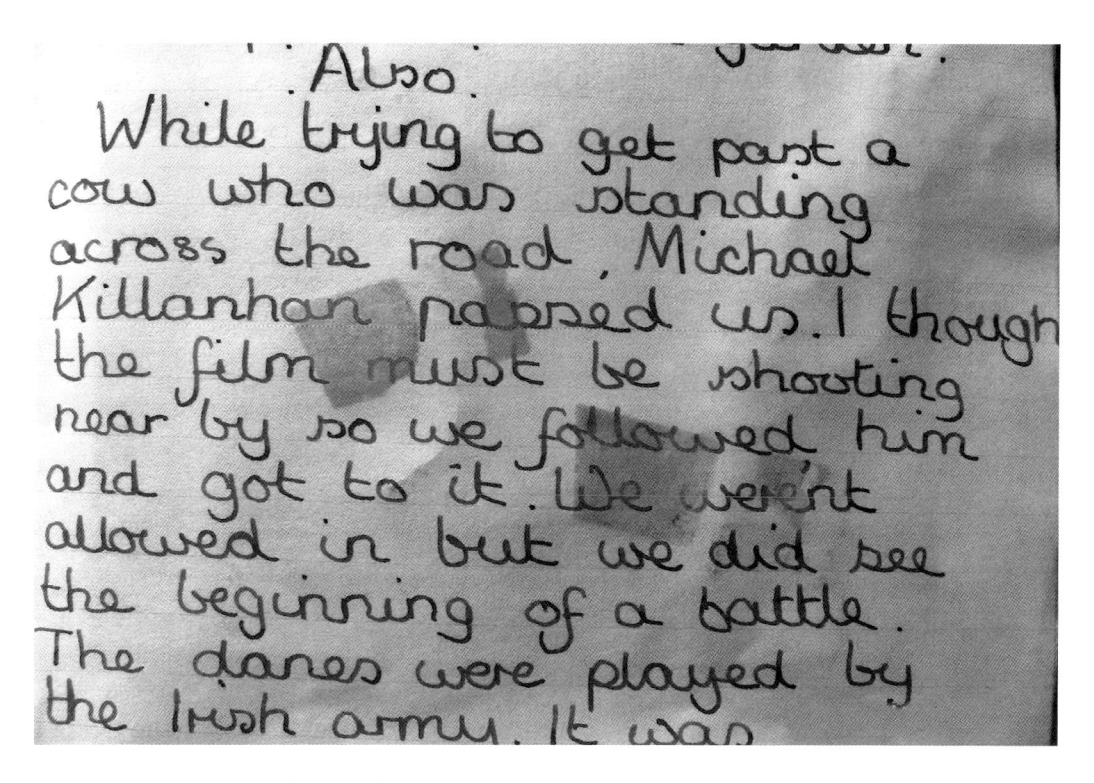

> .Also.
> While trying to get past a cow who was standing across the road, Michael Killanhan passed us. I though the film must be shooting near by so we followed him and got to it. We weren't allowed in but we did see the beginning of a battle. The danes were played by the Irish army. It was

Extract from Sarah Whiting's diary, mentioning Lord Killanin, her father's friend

Lord Killanin, Michael Morris, played a pivotal role in the making of *Alfred The Great*, both in his official role as Associate Producer, as well as in his unofficial ambassadorial capacity as the man who helped make *The Quiet Man* in Cong in 1951, with all of the movie industry sway that that entailed.

His son Redmond also works in the world of motion pictures and was involved with the falcons in *Alfred The Great*. We saw him listed as a 'runner' in one cast/crew list and he also turns up in Sarah Stringer's diary.

Alec Finn of the internationally famous traditional Irish folk group De Dannan worked with the falcons on set too (as we were told by another son of Lord Killanin, Johnny Morris) and he now lives in Oranmore castle, David Hemmings' home during filming in Galway. That De Dannan connection stretches far and wide, not least to Caherlistrane, the home of Dolores Keane. A member of the mighty musical clan (Aunts Sarah, Rita and siblings that include Matt and Sean), she was lead singer with De Dannan in her time and her home place is only a stone's throw from Knockma. An old house at the foot of Knockma, a Protestant chapel in olden times, was actually once home to Dolores' father, Matt.

VIKING SUMMER

The Protestant chapel at the foot of Knockma (© Mary J. Murphy, 1996)

Music swirls around in the very air in north Galway because apart from the Keanes, internationally famous traditional musician Matt Cunningham is from the area too, as is the traditional group, Maigh Seola, plus The Sawdoctors and many others. American country/folk singer, Nanci Griffith, famous for her hit song, *From A Distance,* once called Dolores *"the voice of Ireland",* and those musical tentacles extend to include a transatlantic mix of John Prine, Maura O'Connell, Mary Chapin Carpenter, Emmylou Harris and Nashville producer Jim Rooney. Apart from his vital role in the making of *Alfred The Great*, Lord Killanin was credited with saving the 1980 Olympic Games in Moscow, and the huge turnout at his funeral in 1999 reflected the high esteem in which he had been held. His papers have been deposited in the Tiernan McBride Library in the Irish Film Archive and everybody involved in the film, including the former Mayor of Galway, Bobby Molloy, paid tribute to the hugely positive input he had into its production.

To attach the knowledge and prestige of an international figure like Michael Morris, who had a title given to his family in about 1900 that allowed him to style himself as 'Lord Killanin', was a manifest advantage to the project, particularly in the USA. The movie was in a safe pair of hands under his guidance, never mind the inestimable wealth of his local knowledge. In that respect, as in so many others, MGM had lined its ducks up in a row to ensure the satisfactory outcome of *Alfred The Great.*

Ronnie Burke's photo of David Hemmings on horseback at Ross Lake

CHAPTER TWO

A stellar cast took the lead roles in *Alfred The Great*, led by David Hemmings, then a superstar.

He died on the set of *Samantha's Child* in Romania in December 2003 at 62, having been married four times. He had four sons and two daughters and had enjoyed a diverse career that began when he was a boy soloist, singing in cathedrals the length and breadth of the UK.

VIKING SUMMER

He explained why he accepted the role of Alfred, in the context of the extraordinary success he'd just enjoyed in *Blow-Up*: *"Though the film shoved me into the public eye, there was the distinct chance that I would always be Thomas, the mod photographer, to audiences, no matter what I did in the future. All my roles since then have been conscious attempts to move in new directions. Alfred is different from anything else I have done ...it has not been easy but I have found it rewarding ... I enjoyed the location work in Ireland tremendously. My wife and I rented Oranmore Castle for the summer and we became very involved with the local people."*

His thoughts on himself and on his own life can be read in his autobiography, *Blow Up... and Other Exaggerations,* published after his death, but it's often more instructive to read what others say about a famous person. His death received extensive coverage in all the main English newspapers and it can be gleaned from the numerous obituaries that he had a colourful, not to say chaotic, private life.

He was born in Guildford, Surrey and started his career as a boy soprano, appearing in several works by Benjamin Britten who formed a close friendship with him at the time. Details of that collaboration are described in John Bridcut's *Britten's Children*. Hemmings made his first film appearance in 1954 but it was the mid-sixties before he became famous as a film and pin-up star. He was a slight figure in real life, as many of our extras and Irish participants have told us, almost unnoticeable in a crowd. But something happened when the camera pointed towards him. He responded with an internal charism that shone through perfectly clearly on the screen. There was a marvellous rich Burton-like timbre to his voice, also, which lent a further layer of attractiveness to his screen persona. When Hemmings and the MGM roadshow rolled into Galway, a man called Ronnie Burke was a resident musician in The Sacré Coeur Hotel in Salthill, Galway, and he has marvellous memories from the time. Burke was taken on as a driver of a Mini-Moke van for cameraman Ron Sharpe and was paid a daft amount of money for his pains for months. *"It was a kind of a VW Beetle that had the roof taken off and it was able to have a camera stuck out of the window on each side. It could go across fields and chase after horses for filming."*

Burke's overwhelming recall of that whole mad six months or so while the crew was in Galway was of *"drink everywhere, and parties seven nights a week and the donkey derbies Hemmings hosted in Oranmore Castle on Sunday afternoons."* Hemmings was a bit of a divil, he mused, but a nice man and generous to a fault. Although his last film appearances that

David Hemmings – photo courtesy of MGM promotional literature from 1968

VIKING SUMMER

would have been widely seen were his roles in *Gladiator, Gangs of New York, The League of Extraordinary Gentlemen* with Sean Connery and *Last Orders* (with son Nolan), Hemmings' memory will never clamber out from under the weight of the impact made by *'Blow-Up'* in '66. His *zeitgeist*-capturing role of Thomas, the über-groovy fashion photographer, was seared onto the national consciousness and turned Hemmings into a bona fide star. At one point he co-founded and financed a company called the Hemdale Film Corporation, with John Daly and Derek Gibson and it eventually became well known for the production of *The Terminator (1984), Hoosiers (1986)* and *Platoon,* also from the same year. For much of the 1970s Hemmings was based in Los Angeles working as a director but his cheery ruefulness in *'Last Orders'* shortly before he died was said by one critic to have given tangible presence to the themes of mortality and changing times. He turned into quite a good watercolourist at the end and never dropped the affable and boyish front. This is how Hemmings summed himself up in an extract from his *Telegraph* (Dec 5 2003) obituary: *"I haven't really achieved a great body of outstanding work that can be buffed up and put on the mantelpiece. I've done some real stinkers, and I don't regret any of them because I went into them in the full knowledge that they weren't going to win an Academy award... I don't give a shit about fame. I have no vanity in that department. I don't consider myself to have been a star; I just married some pretty women."* Four, in total.

Up to 1968, Michael York's acting persona had been quite the opposite of the rampaging Viking he played as Guthrum in *Alfred The Great.* He'd been perceived up to that point as a mild-mannered sort of chap and of all of the participants in the film, York appears to have made the most positive lingering impression. This is how he remembered his time spent in Galway as recalled in his autobiography, *Travelling Player.* Returning to London, he said, *"I bought a new MG sports car to speed us to the west of Ireland, where Alfred was to be filmed. In this remote, unchanged corner of furthest Europe it seemed natural that castles should be available for rent."* He continued: *"We leased Creggana Castle, near Galway, an ancient turret set amidst green fields and their patchwork of grey stone walls that had been restored by a French architect with every modern comfort. Meals, however, were still spit-roasted over an open peat fire in the huge stone living room and were often more burnt than King Alfred's legendary cakes! None the less, we delighted in this first romantic 'home'."* York had just married Patrician McCallum and they're still together, 40 years later.

"David Hemmings", said York, *"playing the legendary English king, had rented the even more impressive Oranmore Castle and flew the banner of Wessex from its sea-girt battlements.*

Prunella Ransome, picture courtesy of MGM's publicity material from 1968

VIKING SUMMER

Ronnie Burke's photo of Viking extras, including Frank Deacy, at Ross Lake

Not to be outdone, I raised King Guthrum's Danish standard over mine. One night there was a furious pounding at our massive front door which opened to reveal a posse of locals with faces and accents out of Synge and O'Casey." York quoted the locals: *"'T'wouldn't be the English flag you're after flying there?' one gnarled countenance demanded querulously. Reassured, they shambled off into the moonlight, reminding me that the bigotry and hostility that had killed Behan's hostage were still very much alive..."*

York explained that *"Alfred was filmed either out of doors amidst the local bogs, brays and hills or in a studio complex erected in a local field (Kilchreest) that looked like an Anglo-Saxon theme park with its ancient buildings and modern facilities. It was here that we raped, pillaged and plundered, carrying on exactly as those shocked chroniclers had described to me in the hushed quiet of an Oxford library."* York added more detail about filming on location and a scene that stayed in his mind concerns one in which the crew and

Ronnie Burke's photo of Michael York on horseback at Ross Lake

cast were at Killinure. *"In one thrilling sequence we used the River Shannon as the Viking 'swan-road' over which their longships came swooping ashore. Exact replicas of the Gokstadt ship, they were immensely seaworthy. Indeed, some hardy fool was planning to sail one to America as a publicity stunt – presumably using the Vinland map for guidance! We also employed a contingent of the Irish army as extras so that, in the quaint ways of this singular nation, many had their first taste of warfare using spears and battleaxes. Most spent their time lolling on sword and sward, blond wigs outrageously askew, looking for all the world like drag queens on a day trip."* The weather at the time, said York in *Travelling Player*, was magnificent. *"The best summer since 1922, according to the locals. So instead of the wild, windblown skies the film-makers had hoped for, we had an uninterrupted Mediterranean blue."* York concluded: *"Later, I was able to confirm a correlation between Pat's and my presence and the weather. I hardly dare tempt providence by saying so, but fine weather seems to follow us wherever we go. I even became an adept*

VIKING SUMMER

Ronnie Burke's photo of Clive Donner directing from above, on the Cam-El, (camera elevator) at Ross Lake

horseman, although my enthusiasm remained as skin-deep as the bruises sustained from being involuntarily catapulted over stone walls in mid-gallop."

Prunella Ransome didn't leave such a distinct written impression from her involvement in *Alfred The Great* and in fact it's difficult to track her career at all. Apart from a few appearances in televison shows like *Heartbeat*, she didn't turn up in too many credits after *Alfred*. She was born in Croydon, England, in 1943, died in 2003, and was nominated for a Golden Globe during her career.

Ronnie Burke's photo of Asst Dir. Peter Price in the foreground at Ross lake

Her role in *Alfred The Great* followed her success as Fanny Robin in *Far From The Madding Crowd* from 1967, in which she appeared with Hemmings.

Ian, now Sir Ian, McKellen having been knighted in 1990, had the most extraordinary stage career for years before he took to the screen. Now, he's one of the most famous actors in the world, in the wake of his appearances as Gandalf in *The Lord of the Rings* movies. He invited us to use whatever we wished from his webpage, which we did.

VIKING SUMMER

Sir Ian McKellen, as Roger the bandit, in a coracle at Ross Lake

One item is a fine picture of Sir Ian in a coracle paddling along by the banks of a river and that one was taken at Ross Lake, as were Ronnie Burke's own photographs. McKellen said about the film: *"I was a bandit fighting with Alfred against the Viking invasion. My mate was played by Vivien Merchant, Mrs. Harold Pinter."* With regard to his swordsmanship skills, he explained that *"I was trained on the spot in Galway to do the fairly primitive broadsword fighting of the battle scenes. I was advised to use Errol Flynn's trick when mortally wounded – look surprised."* The fighting extras were supplied by the Irish army, he said, just as their predecessors had fought in Laurence Olivier's film, *Richard III,* in the early 1950s."

Ian McKellen was born in Burnley, Lancashire, England, on May 25 1939 and made his professional debut in 1965 in *A Touch Of Love*. He has been directing plays since the mid-1960s and has received the prestigious Olivier award five times. He's a stage man, more than a movie guy, but his recent appearances in modern films like *Harry Potter* and the *Lord of the Rings* trilogy have brought him to the attention of a younger audience who would have scant interest in his theatrical work.

Jim Norton played Thanet in *Alfred The Great* and actually joined the RTE Rep on the same

Dear Mary Murphy

You will find some photographs and commentary on ALFRED THE GREAT in the film section of www.mckellen.com. You are welcome to use anything there.

best wishes

Ian McKellen

Sir Ian McKellen's note sent during the research for this book.

day as Henry Comerford back in the mid 1950s. Some fifty years later, Norton won a Tony Award in New York in June 2008 for his role in *The Seafarer*. Colin Blakely, who played Asher in *Alfred*, died in 1986 and was a well-known British character actor from Bangor in County Down. Peter Vaughan would be well known to those who recall the 1970s English television series, *Porridge* because he played Grouty in that show. In *Alfred*, his role was that of Burrud. Then a 19-year-old unknown ingénue, Sinead Cusack played Edith in this, her debut film in 1968, and was Prunella Ransome's maid. Cusack comes from a distinguished family of actors and has played leading Shakespearean roles in RSC and Royal Court productions of *Macbeth*, as Lady Macbeth.

She kicked off her career in the 1960s with a move to London from her native Dublin and soon thereafter began her career with the RSC. After *Alfred The Great*, she starred opposite Peter Sellers in the small comedy, *Hoffman*. For the best part of the next two decades she concentrated her efforts on the stage and made her Broadway debut in 1984 opposite Derek Jacobi in the repertory productions (of the RSC) – *Much Ado About Nothing* and *Cyrano de Bergerac*, earning a Tony nomination for her work as Beatrice in the former. Born to Cyril Cusack and his wife Máirín, in Dublin's Dalkey, Sinead Moira has two brothers (Padraig and Paul) and made her stage debut in *The Importance of Mr. O* in Dublin as a 12-year-old. She then attended the Holy Child Convent in Killiney, Dublin, and went on to University College Dublin. Her career has been remarkably consistent and weighted heavily towards the theatre, but she did make her television debut in 1970 playing Emily to her father's Barkis in a British

VIKING SUMMER

Ronnie Burke's photo of the clapper board used for scenes at Ross lake

production of *David Copperfield*. She also worked with her father (as well as with her two acting sisters, Niamh and Sorcha) in a West End 1990 production of *The Three Sisters*. Married to Jeremy Irons, she acted with him in 1996 when she appeared alongside Liv Tyler in Bertolucci's *Stealing Beauty*. At the time of writing Miss Cusack was appearing on Broadway in Tom Stoppard's play, *Rock and Roll*, and she telephoned from London the evening before taking off for that run in New York in the winter of 2007. Her memories of *Alfred* were humorous and brief. Apart from explaining that it wasn't a succesful picture she recalled that her lines were eventually cut down to one or two in the final edit and remembered that

```
                                        April 1968   33
   54   Continued                                      54
                     ALFRED  David Hemmings
            Look at the moon ... you see it?
                 (she nods)
            How does it change its shape from day to day?

                     AELHSWITH  Prunella Ransom
            You should ask your wise man.

                     ALFRED
            Asher?  He says the ancients never agreed.
            I told him to find the answer for me, but he
            never will.
                 (moves on)
            We'll go to Rome to find a thing like that ...

                     AELHSWITH
            When do you mean to make this pilgrimage?
            Is it in earnest?

     Alfred nods.  They have reached the wall of the strongpoint
     Alfred leans against it, stroking the falcon's head.
```

Extract from an actual page of script from *Alfred The Great*, which was one of the many treasures contained in Sarah (Stringer) Whiting's diary from 1968. It refers to a scene where Hemmings and Ransome are admiring a falcon

Hemmings had to say terribly rude things to her in one of her few surviving scenes. She remembered, too, Belclare and the hill of Knockma, as well as the sports day she attended (in Ballyglunin) but most of her remaining memories have evaporated into the mists of the past.

When a film divebombs, as *Alfred The Great* did, one of the easiest culprits to point a finger at is the screen writer. In this case, James R. Webb would be one of those primarily responsible for the dialogue in the script and as we can see from the extracts of the actual script (embedded in the pages of Sarah Stringer Whiting's diary from 1968), some of it was rum stuff indeed and almost impossible to say with a straight face.

On MGM's own promotional material the two men credited with the screenplay are Ken Taylor and James R. Webb and it had been knocking around for a few years because we saw mention of it being sent to Lord Killanin in May 1964 – 139 pages typewritten on A4 paper. It should have been a fine script because Webb was an alumnus (according to Hal Erikson of *All Movie Guide*) of Stanford University and was a prolific magazine writer when he

VIKING SUMMER

Photo of swords and knives used in 'Alfred the Great', given to us by Muiris O'Faoláin of Moycullen National School. These film props were donated to the school by Faherty Coaches who provided transport facilities to MGM during the making of the film.

entered the world of films in 1939. After an apprenticeship with Republic's western and serial units, he moved to the big league at Warner Brothers and then spent a few years with Hecht-Hill-Lancaster, penning many Burt Lancaster vehicles in the 1950s. Afterwards he collaborated on some marvellous Gregory Peck films and the point we're banging home here with total lack of subtlety is that the man knew how to write for films and was a well respected, hugely experienced professional, not some dodgy hack. That duck was lined up properly too. For his work on *Cape Fear*, he was nominated in 1962 for a Best Original Screenplay award. And yet Alfred sank under the weight, partially, of its own verbal pomposity.

The music is the first striking aspect of *Alfred The Great* that we notice because the actual rolling credits at the opening are a bit scant and amateurish-looking. The synopsis at the beginning that's meant to entice us and get us prepared to be enthralled is a bit suspect too, apparently devised for seven-year-olds, but the music is melodiously bombastic from the very start. The man primarily responsible for that was Raymond Leppard.

He was born in London in 1927, grew up in Bath and studied harpsichord and viola at Cambridge University. We can see quite clearly from the above that the production crew and acting stock in the film were from the top drawer and if they weren't to blame for the eventual distaster that unfolded, perhaps the locations were ill chosen. Could that have been what went so terribly wrong? Not alone may it have been the wrong film at the wrong time, but could *Alfred The Great* have conceivably been located in the wrong place too?

CHAPTER THREE

Much time, effort, energy and expense were expended on choosing the precise locations that Killanin, Donner, Smith and Stringer thought best exemplified the 'look' they hoped to achieve for their ninth-century epic. The rough terrain of the Slieve Aughtys, the bleakly beautiful Ross Lake region and the immutable statuesque lump that is the hill of Knockma were carefully included to attain that vision. Historians had delved on behalf of Bernard Smith and dug out all available references to Alfred's Wessex of the 870s, and the west of Ireland suited their purposes. The rugged terrain plus the usual grey, overcast, drizzly weather were exactly what were required. Of course the Lord Killanin connection was the obvious cinematic magnet that drew MGM to Ireland. The excitement – and revenue – generated by the making of John Ford's *The Quiet Man,* with Lord Killanin in close attendance in the Cong region in 1951, was still a vibrant memory.

Another who believes that Galway connections contributed to the setting of *Alfred The Great* in the county is David Barrett of Edward Holdings. He explained, *"A family member of mine was instrumental in the fact that Galway was chosen as its location. His name was Sean Barrett and he was originally from Abbeygate Street. He was the founder and General Secretary of the Film Artistes Association which looked after the extras during filming, and had worked in the movie industry in the UK from the end of the Second World War. He was close to many of the players in it and was close too to John Huston and Peter O'Toole and a famous stuntman called Peter Perkins, who would all have encouraged the production on location in Galway".*

Much tremendous historical research and writing has been done on Castlehackett and its environs by (Caherlistrane born but Dublin-based) Michael J. Hughes and anyone with sufficient interest in the Kirwans of Castlehackett should get their hands on his books. A newer book about the area has been written – Ronan Lynch's *The Kirwans of Castlehackett,* and it would have been immensely instructive for Lord Killanin and Co in 1968. Keeping the rich seam of history mined in the locality are Kieran and Padraig Reaney, who assist in producing the local Caherlistrane-Kilcoona newsletter (www.caherlistrane-kilcoona), done in conjunction with the Community Council chaired by Brendan Gannon, under the guiding hand of parish priest Fr. Pat O'Brien, a poet, writer and broadcaster. Gannon was himself an extra in *Alfred The Great* along with neighbours like Joe Flanagan. Kieran Reaney in particular has an immense interest in the film, has written about it frequently and gathered some

VIKING SUMMER

Fr. Pat O'Brien, parish priest in Caherlistrane

Extract from Sarah Whiting's diary, referring to the perch caught in Lough Hackett when they stayed in Lisdonagh house as guests of Mrs. V. Palmer

names for us of those who were involved. They include Thomas Costello from Mossfort, Peter Corcoran from Caherlistrane, Martin Kavanagh, Eamon Hughes, Owen McGagh and Paddy Joe Higgins.

Stunning scenes shot at Lough Corrib feature in glorious Technicolor in *Alfred The Great*, and the 552-foot-high hill of Knockma (scene of the major Battle of White Horse Hill) is in Belclare, actually in the parish of Corofin. The hinterland of the mini-mountain, loosely known as Maigh Seola in the annals of old, contains another smaller lake, minuscule in comparison with the Corrib, Lough Hackett (called after the Hackett Anglo-Norman family who had the land in the 13th century). It turned up in Sarah Whiting's schoolgirl diary that she kept during the summer of 1968 when she was on holidays with her father, Set Designer, Michael Stringer. They'd visited Valda Palmer of Lisdonagh House, adjacent to Lough Hackett.

The crannóg in the middle of Lough Hackett dates back perhaps a thousand years and Oscar Wilde's father, William, described it as the best example of its type in the entire Lough Corrib catchment area.

The hill of Knockma has drawn people towards it since prehistoric times and was famed in annals and stories long before the current modern grave from the 1950s was placed there. That belongs to Lieutenant - General Denis Bernard, known locally as 'The General', a former Governor of Bermuda just before WWII began in 1939. He came back to live in Castlehackett when he retired, and died in

LOUGH HACKET
Loċ Cıme

LOUGH HACKETT, Caherlistrane, adjacent to Lisdonagh House. It was the venue for a fishing party, guests of Valda Palmer, in August of 1968 that included Set Designer Michael Stringer and others. Apparently some perch were caught, according to notes kept in the diary of then 12-year-old Sarah (Stringer) Whiting

1956. That's an event that many older people in the community, including Mick and Mary Glynn of Feeragh, recall to this day because the coffin had to be hauled up in a tractor and trailer to the top of Knockma for burial. After General Bernard's death the estate passed to his nephew, Percy Paley and when he died in 1985 the three-hundred-year-old Kirwan line came to an end. Philip Jones currently occupies the house.

In our own time it's been used as a film location for the making of an Australian children's serial, *Foreign Exchange,* and the students of Castlehackett school are fascinated by the 'portal' method of transport used by the leads in the show – Brett from Australia and Hannah from Galway - Castlehackett House being portrayed as a girls' boarding school in the programme. It was co-produced by Magma Films who are based in Galway and *Foreign Exchange* was actually back on our TV screens in August 2008.

Knockma is by far the most prominent landmark in the broad area that straddles the border between north Galway and south Mayo and was a stunning location for shooting scenes from the film. Lord Killanin and his MGM counterparts chose wisely and well when they opted to co-opt it, temporarily, for their cinematic purposes, with the magnificence of Croagh Patrick glowering down from the north some forty miles away.

VIKING SUMMER

Castlehackett House (photo © Mary J. Murphy 2008)

With locations chosen, time then to move on to the hundreds of props required, all of which were beautifully made - swords, shields, braziers, tables, chairs, thrones and so on. A primary school principal in Moycullen, Maurice Whelan, told us that some of those very props from the film have been donated to his school by Faherty's Coaches, items that had been abandoned in their buses after filming had been completed. Whatever went awry, it wasn't the fault of the fantastically crafted props. Perhaps, then, MGM were bad paymasters? Mean? Diliatory in reimbursing participants for their trouble? Maybe enough cash wasn't released to lubricate the wheels of commerce? But that can't be the reason for the movie's flop either because we came across person after person who said that so all-pervasive were the big fat wads of crisp brand-new pound notes being waved about the place that MGM was colloquially known far and wide as *'Money Gone Mad'.*

In the unit lists and notes we saw from the movie, there are scores upon scores of people listed as active participants in the production (250 approx), from the director to Redmond Morris, Donner's personal assistant (and Lord Killanin's son), and on to the hairdressers and their assistants, carpenters, chefs, maintenance people and so forth. The mind aches at the extent of the logistics, never mind the bill that must have been run up to pay for that. The typewritten notes and call sheets, many of them signed by Lord Killanin, are all perfectly preserved and models of clarity, and illustrate the scale of the project. We've not come across a bottom line figure anywhere that we can say was the actual cost to MGM of making the film but as £4 million sterling was bandied about a lot, we'll go with that. The payment system

Corrib Crafts employees, Michael Tierney, Joe Kelly, Michael Lally

VIKING SUMMER

Corrib Crafts employees, John Daly and Charley Lynch

for the hundreds of extras involved was hugely complicated - there were permanent ones and part-time ones and day-extras and 'wet pay' and 'waiting pay' and so forth - but all of those to whom we spoke are still tickling themselves forty years later at the soft money they picked up for sport. John Morris from Caltra, Belclare, worked on the set with a tractor and trailer all during the summer and recalls quite clearly that he got £84 for his first week's work with MGM. That was at a time when the average weekly pay was in the order of £16-£18. John gave twenty to his father – which ran the car for a month – and twenty to his mother, which ran the house for a month, and used the remainder for his own enjoyment! John further recalls the mountain of cash arriving at Knockma in a big bulging suitcase every Friday, out from the Bank of Ireland in Galway, with two men riding shotgun alongside it. Money doesn't appear to have been an object to the initial proceedings, except perhaps towards the end when the budget went AWOL.

Tom Dowd of Corrib Crafts remembers that he was eventually able to buy a brand-new Mini Minor for himself back then that cost the best part of £400. Apart from all of the timber work he made in Al O'Dea's premises in Tuam, Tom also twisted about ten miles of straw rope by hand with his father for the film. He didn't complain about reimbursement either, nor did Al O'Dea, who managed to buy a new VW Beetle for himself too, after striking a more than satisfactory deal with Michael Stringer and the relevant film personnel. So, it looks like parsimony didn't sink the good ship *Alfred*, either. The extras and others employed by the company lined up on the side of the hill each week, often in blazing hot sunshine, and queued for their payment. This long snaking line often contained the unexpected yet imposing figure of Lord Killanin, who had warned Henry Comerford earlier to beware of the

Corrib Crafts, MGM employee, M. Tierney, C. Lynch and J. Kelly

fly-by-night nature of film productions. They could go "smash!" overnight, he warned the young solicitor, so better get paid cash in hand on a regular basis. The good Lord proceeded to practise what he preached, leading by example.

Extras got between £7 and £14 per day, depending on their skills level and what was required from them on any particular day of shooting. Children (including Mary Murphy Callanan) from Kilchreest, recall being offered a red ten shilling note for every live frog and crow they could catch and bring to the production crew for certain scenes. Willie Cunningham from Biggera, Belclare, worked with the production moving the timber rostrums (for the cameras) from place to place at

Corrib Crafts, unknown woman with Al O'Dea

39

VIKING SUMMER

Castlehackett and he remembers that he got a hayturner afterwards, courtesy of MGM. Of course, the implement was known forever after as *'Alfred's* Hayturner'.

Tom Dowd's Mini has gone on to the great scrapyard in the sky but he's still making exquisite furniture on his own premises in Kilconly today and said that some of his bed designs are influenced by items he made for the film forty years ago. He has an immensely clear recall of the first day Michael Stringer walked into the Corrib Craft premises in Tuam, Dowd having known nothing about *Alfred The Great* up to that point.

"At the time," said Dowd, *"there were probably about six lads and the boss, Al O'Dea, working there. We were doing all right but weren't too busy. What we were doing was trying to revive old style Irish furniture. Al O'Dea himself had the idea. He wasn't a carpenter but he was a great man for ideas."* The steady pace in the craft shop was abandoned once the agreement was made with Stringer because the firm undertook to make all of the timber furnishings that would be needed for the movie. *"The full capacity of our workshop was in use for two months or more,"* explained Tom, *"and Stringer had another man with him when he came in, Norman Dorme, I think. Stringer we found to be a very nice man to deal with, very easy to get on with. It was rather odd, really,"* laughed Dowd, *"as Michael Stringer had to get it into our heads that he wanted all this stuff crooked! 'Wobbly', that was a great word of his. The fellas in the workshop used to say 'Wobbly is coming again' every time Stringer arrived."*

All the joints had to be jimmied open loosely in the tabletops and the chairs and the wardrobes, creating gaps to make them look old. A lot of the stuff was made outdoors, in the front yard, and there was a higher wall there at the time, and a small gate in the front. *"So you can imagine,"* smiled Tom, *"the interest of the local people when they saw these huge 9 foot tent poles appearing up over the top of the wall. It was a great attraction and The Tuam Herald newspaper was down nearly every week. I'm sure Jim Fahy was down there, and Jim Carney too, as well as a photographer called Michael Shaughnessy."*

Jim Carney of *The Tuam Herald* and *RTE* has written extensively about the making of the film, having participated in it as an 18-year old extra who had just done his Leaving Certificate that year. The summer was his own before he took up his post as a trainee journalist in *The Tuam Herald.*

Corrib Crafts, Al O'Dea, MGM employee, M. Tierney, C. Lynch

As far as Tom Dowd was concerned, Kilchreest was where the action was. *"That was what we all wanted to see,"* he said, *"the MGM studio complex, but we had no business going up there unless we had to deliver something. I remember seeing this lovely big round tower and going around the back of it, and nothing there! There was a full village like that and the tower looked just like the real one here in Kilbannon now."*

Dowd's description of Michael Stringer was concise - *"He was a very ordinary kind of guy, of average build and spoke very quietly. Mannerly and easy to work with. He told us what he wanted and had a few pictures and some drawings with him."* On that first day he told them that the work they'd make was going to be for a film, a big film, that was going to be a big deal in the area and was going to be filmed locally. Corrib Crafts was the nearest place that had the capacity to make the kind of furniture the MGM crew wanted. *"He said if we were prepared to do things the way he wanted to do it, there was a lot of work and money there."* To the best of Tom Dowd's memory, the men who were with him in Corrib Crafts then

VIKING SUMMER

Original interior drawings of Abbott from Alfred The Great

were Peter Bugg, a nephew of Al O'Dea's, now working as a woodwork teacher in America, John Daly, Charlie Lynch and Joe Kelly. It's a very delicate business, talking to people about money and payment, even if forty years have lapsed in the interim, but from what we can gather, Corrib Crafts was "fairly paid" for the work they did. *"Al O'Dea came up with the prices and they – Stringer and Co – were generally OK about it. We were told there was something like four million pounds sterling being spent on the film and there was no problem with money. Payment was in Irish pounds and the cheques came in. The hardest thing all the way through was for us to do things the way they wanted the work done - badly. It went against our training completely and was very, very hard to do."*

Dowd was the foreman of their small group and they worked from blueprints that Stringer and the production team provided. The film company also supplied the wood, *"this very special light stuff, I think the name was 'balsa', and it was designed to cause as few injuries and as little damage as possible in the middle of action scenes. It was nearly as light as aeroboard and we made almost everything for the film out of it. We certainly made the thrones for the two kings because I personally made them myself and then the final carving on them was done by a man named Albert O'Toole in Galway. I think he also did the carving*

Original exterior 'piglets' sketch of the medieval village built at Kilchreest

of the figure that eventually turned into the bronze bust of John F. Kennedy in Eyre Square."

Michael Stringer was on site in Corrib Crafts nearly every day, as well as Norman Dorme. Clive Donner was in and out a few times too. Tom Dowd hasn't any great recall of Donner, apart from the fact that he seemed to be a quiet man – as lots of people have told us – but his impression of Stringer was that he was a man who paid great attention to detail. That aspect of his personality came across very strongly in the many things that were said about him in various obituaries we came across following his death in 2004, his acute one-hundred-per-cent focus on the job in hand.

When he saw the film after it was released Dowd was a disappointed man. It was slow-moving and hardly any of Corrib Crafts' items could be seen in the picture. *"You couldn't see much of our furniture at all and you couldn't see much of the ten miles of hay ropes we made either."* Tom used to get 25 yards into a roll of rope, then put three rolls into a bag and then put three bags into the Mini boot every morning and hit off to Tuam from Kilconly. He used to stack the bags up beside the wall at Corrib Crafts and the MGM lorry would come and pick them up as required.

VIKING SUMMER

```
                    Concrete       ACCESS  ROAD

              "ALFRED THE GREAT"
          MAIN SETS ·IN LOCATION STUDIO
   INTERIOR SETS                    EXTERIOR
   INT: ST. JOHN'S CHURCH    AND   ABBEY YARD - FIELDS & VILLAGE
   INT: ST MARY'S CONVENT    AND   FIELDS
   INT: ETHELRED'S & ALFRED'S PALACE AND COURTYARD
   INT: ETHELRED'S CORRIDOR }
         A GUEST ROOM       }
   INT: ETHELRED'S BEDROOM
   INT: GUTHRUM'S GREAT HALL     }
   AND CORRIDOR TO AELSWITH'S ROOM }
   INT: AELSWITH'S BEDROOM  AND  CIRCULAR STAIRS & CASTLE GATES
   INT: CASTLE CHAPEL  AND    "     "      "   "   "
   INT: BUHRUDS ROOM (RV)         EXT: ALFRED'S GARDEN
   INT: ALFRED'S HUT C.U. etc
```

The picture lists the scenes/locations that were based at the MGM Complex at Kilchreest

The real giveaway as to who, locally, was getting a few bob from the film crowd, was beards. He mentioned Pake Byrne and Joe Dillon and indeed my own husband has recall of local men like Joe Cunningham from Feeragh, with a beard, as well as his uncle, Joe Moran, from Manusflynn. Dowd said the same thing, explaining that hardly anyone from the area ever wore one until Alfred came along. David Burke, editor of *The Tuam Herald*, remembers talk of beards too, even though he had no hands-on role in the movie. *"I was an exchange student in France that summer, hence not involved, but I do remember there was a beard-growing competition in Tuam Youth Club."* He also has memories of speaking with O'Dea about Corrib Crafts' woodwork for the film, and Jim Norton was the judge of that very same beard-growing competition.

The security in Castlehackett was tight enough, Tom said, and there was really no way in the main gate unless you had a pass or a good reason to be there. That explains why photos are quite scarce from that time because allowing for the fact that cameras weren't as common then as they are now, security precluded people from taking unflattering 'snaps' of the stars. MGM's coffers were well stretched that summer and another who benefited from their largesse was Michael Mullery, Galway Auctioneer. He was only a slip of a lad in 1968 and participated in the film with his now deceased father, Joe, as well as with a man called Paddy

Original exterior sketch of medieval village built at Kilchreest (Courtesy of A.R. Smith)

Delaney from Abbeyknockmoy. Both of the older men worked on the movie all through the summer and Michael recalls seeing all of the secondary school students from Tuam who joined on set as extras once the summer holidays came in July of that year. Burke's Buses ferried the crowds to and fro (and indeed Maurice Burke of Burke's Buses confirmed for us that his parents were involved with the film production on a transport basis), and Michael had no difficulty recalling his financial remuneration for his acting troubles. *'We got seven crispy pound notes every day,"* Mullery said, *"and they used to leave it on the table in front of us on the hill in Belclare."* His memories of the food on location remain equally clear. *"It was fabulous,"* he said, *"just fabulous"* and was much enjoyed by the lads from CBS and St. Jarlath's. *"Some of them were in and out of the location, depending on requirements, for four or five days and then they were gone again."* Mr Mullery himself was involved as an extra for eight or ten days and recalled that the man who did the hiring and firing was *"Spince, and the only other thing I can remember clearly from the time was the heat – the sun was cracking the stones."*

A son of Willie Cunningham from Biggera at the foothills of Castlehackett hill, Dr. John, lectures in history in NUIG and he told us that he has a 'haphazard recall' of the film,

VIKING SUMMER

primarily because he was only ten years old at the time. One of the stronger memories he has is of his father coming home in the evening with pockets full of sweets and chocolate after a day's filming. Willie Cunningham was involved in the production for some weeks with his tractor and trailer and is now in his 91st year. Along with his wife, Mary, he laughed as he recalled the wonderfully exciting time when Hollywood came to the hill. Nothing like it had ever been seen in the area and Willie said that the weight of the rostrums he had to load, move and unload every day, regularly caused the front of the tractor to lift up slightly in the air. Burgers are another strong memory and he ate so many that he hasn't eaten another since!

The man he worked for was Frank Wardale, a supervising electrician with MGM. Others whom Mr. Cunningham recalls from the locality include Joe Flanagan from Cave, Caherlistrane; Micky Fox from Glenrevagh; Tommy Hession from Ballydotia; Sean O'Brien of Carheens, Tim Lawless from Anbally, John Morris from Caltragh and Bernie Henihan, his brother-in-law. When viewing *Alfred The Great* at this remove, there is no feeling of puzzlement as to why certain locations were chosen, and there's no jarringly unsuitable scene that screams "bad choice!" The four main places picked for filming appear eminently scenic and do not, we feel sure, constitute an excuse for the flop.

CHAPTER FOUR

Wheels had been turning for years before any visible sign of MGM's substantial production appeared in Castlehackett in 1968 and an awful lot of money had been spent before a camera was switched on. The onus for the organising of the legal end of things, on behalf of the film company, fell onto the shoulders of Henry Comerford. He explains in the foreword of this book how his father's firm came to be involved in the project as the company's legal representative and John Morris of Caltragh told us that his own father had been sworn to secrecy about aspects of the film nearly two years before the elaborate cinematic convoy rolled onto Knockma. Absolutely nothing had been left to chance by MGM's 'advance patrol'.

Then, by golly, all hell broke loose and the high-jinks began in earnest. In a nutshell, "Galway went mad," laughed Henry Comerford. He was there from day one when a production man (whose name has slid from his memory) walked into his father's practice in Galway and produced the script of the movie. Mr Comerford, using delicately couched language, made it abundantly clear to this representative from MGM that he felt that perhaps the script wasn't quite the finished article, but to no avail. He was told in no uncertain terms that matters had to proceed, dodgy script notwithstanding, as such an enormous amount of money had already been spent.

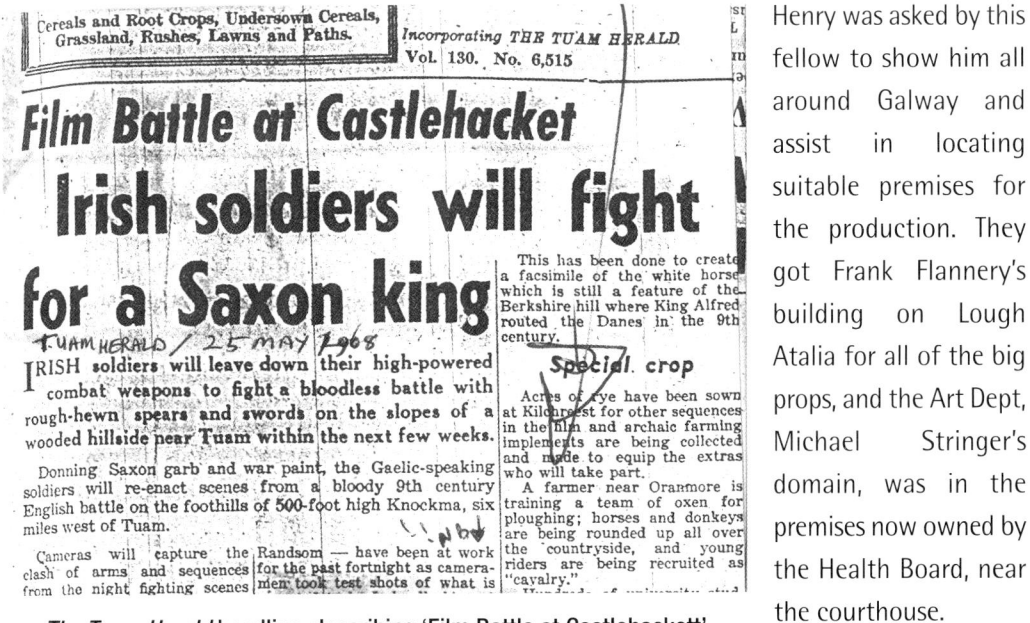

Henry was asked by this fellow to show him all around Galway and assist in locating suitable premises for the production. They got Frank Flannery's building on Lough Atalia for all of the big props, and the Art Dept, Michael Stringer's domain, was in the premises now owned by the Health Board, near the courthouse.

The Tuam Herald headline, describing 'Film Battle at Castlehackett'

VIKING SUMMER

> M.G.M. BRITISH STUDIOS, LTD.,
> c/o Flannery's Buildings, Lough Atalia Road, Galway.
>
> Dear Mr Barrett,
>
> Re: "ALFRED THE GREAT"
>
> We acknowledge receipt of your communication/application re: the above film
>
> This is receiving our attention.
>
> ~~We regretfully are unable to offer you a position on our production.~~
>
> Yours faithfully,
>
> M.G.M. BRITISH STUDIOS, LTD.,
>
> HUGH HARLOW,
> *Unit Manager.*

Original receipt for people applying to be extras on the movie, showing MGM's temporary address at the Flannery buildings at Lough Atalia, Galway.
(Receipt courtesy of Pat Barrett, Loughrea)

Photo of Pat Barrett, Loughrea, an extra in the film

Michael's widow, Layne Stringer, told us that Michael had lived and worked in a studio in East Sussex owned by a Victorian painter, Val Princeps, in his latter years and although he was not quite as well known as his friend, Rossetti, Mr. Stringer had great pleasure in working in a space so closely associated with other fellow artists. All of the colour drawings we have from the storyboards were painted by Michael Stringer, who worked at great speed and was highly prolific, and who would have been horrified at the contemporary use of computer-generated graphics in films, likening them, perhaps, to an elaborate version of 'painting by numbers'. Layne Stringer passed away in July 2008 and we are grateful for the beautifully ornate jewel-like paintings from the film, done by Mr. Stringer, that she sent us, which complement the storyboard sketches done by artists John Bodimeade and John Rose.

Henry Comerford glanced through the cast and crew list of *Alfred The Great* when we met in his home on the shores of Lough Corrib and practically every name prompted an anecdote from the past. His recall of forty-year-old events was startlingly clear. He is an actor and a playwright and a writer, with many substantial legal tomes to his name. He worked with the Radio Eireann Rep in Dublin in the 1950s, alongside Jim Norton whom Comerford knew as "Jimmy." Contemporaries of both men in Dublin back then would have included Brendan Behan, Paddy Kavanagh and the literary like, plus actors in the Rep like Chris Curran, Peg Monaghan, Niall Toibin, Benny Caldwell, Daphne Carroll, Eithne Dunne and Archie O'Sullivan. The money, dare we descend to such vulgar depths and mention it in the same breath as 'The Arts', was good in the Rep too, being something in the order of £12 pounds weekly, at a time when the Abbey was paying only an equivalent £8. Contrast that with the silly money the extras got in *Alfred The Great* just ten years later and we begin to see why the movie, dud and all as it was, left such an extraordinary impression on all who were involved at a financial level.

The entire film scenario was totally over the top in every respect, Comerford said, but he also explained that it meant a monumental amount of work for his firm. All of the lettings had to be sorted, and arrangements for the studio in Kilchreest were horrendously complicated, partly because of the insistence of Bernard Smith (Producer and He Who Must be Obeyed) in inserting all kinds of covenants. He wanted, explained Henry, to return the location to the owners in precisely the same condition as it was before the film company arrived. That was next to impossible and hugely expensive. A lengthy process was undertaken to ensure that all involved would be properly compensated, and MGM would be exonerated from restoring the property to its original condition. On another occasion Comerford recalled being involved in negotiations with seven farmers at the one time when the film crew was out near Ross Lake in Roscahill, between Moycullen and Oughterard. *"Everywhere the film company set a foot down meant legal work to sort things out."*

Hemmings wasn't the most popular of actors and there was an incident in Kilchreest when a quiet horse had to be chosen for him for a publicity photoshoot for an American magazine. Someone (and Omerta surrounds the culprit to this day) swopped the quiet beast for a friskier one, with the result that Hemmings unexpectedly ended up on his tailboard. There are yarns too, of the wild, wild parties that he held in Oranmore Castle and there was the infamous night when his jaw and/or teeth 'got' broken in the castle. People have told us that they're convinced that Hemmings got a belt or two on the jaw for being overly amorous towards women who weren't his wife while others are adamant that it was a genuine accident. He

VIKING SUMMER

fell whilst attempting to climb the battlements during a ridiculous bout of tomfoolery, prompted by an excessive intake of alcohol. His injury made the pages of the *Irish Times*, such was the to-do that swirled around the incident. The bean-counters and the money men must have been having collective hissy-fits because the whole project revolved around Hemmings. His indisposition caused major alarm and pushed the increasingly precarious budgetary situation even farther out of control and off into the wild blue yonder.

Henry Comerford wasn't there that night and has no idea of what actually happened but he does remember laughing like a drain on discovering that Prunella Ransome continued filming, talking to a wall (Hemmings' stand-in), while the star himself was actually whisked off to have his jaw set. The film company was in terrible trouble over the delay - it would cost serious money to shoot around Hemmings, and then there was always the danger that his teeth and jaw, post-hospitalisation, wouldn't match the jaw and teeth that had already been filmed, wrapped and placed in the can.

Mr. Comerford allowed that even though Hemmings was as mad as a hatter, he had a wonderful speaking voice and was quite a good actor. A high point for many Galwegians during the making of the film was the fund-raising show that was held in town over two nights (23 and 24 August 1968) in aid of the Mayor's fund for Biafra. Hemmings was MC for the occasion, Bobby Molloy was mayor at the time and other MGM stars who participated were Sinead Cusack, Jim Norton, Michael York, Julian Chagrin and Christopher Timothy. It took place in the Rosary Hall in Taylor's Hill.

The stars mingled with local talent and the programme consisted of various dramatic excerpts, gymnastics, mime, singing and dancing. After his two-night MC stint, Hemmings then went on to referee the challenge game of soccer between the film staff and extras from the battle scenes. The game took place at the Grammar School and the local bunch was captained by Ciaran Keys, the Irish Universities and UCG goalkeeper, and he was joined by three members of the UCG team which won the Collingwood cup. Names from that team include N. Walsh, J. Varley, S. Heaney, C. Duggan, S. Conway, G. O'Beirne, D. Geraghty, F. Deacy (whom we caught up with in Canada and Clare, forty years later), J. Fahy and T. Davin. All of these extra-curricular activities serve to illustrate that MGM played the PR game smoothly and kept the whole town 'on side' during filming, which in tandem with the exquisitely detailed legal arrangements, ensured that ruffled feathers were kept to an absolute minimum. So, neither of those two elements contributed to the downfall of the film either.

The Filming of MGM's 'Alfred The Great' in Galway in 1968

From left to right: Clive Donner, Robert Molloy and Lord Killanin (picture courtesy of R. Molloy)

From left to right: Bernard Smith, Robert Molloy and Clive Donner (picture courtesy of R. Molloy)

VIKING SUMMER

Christy Dooley's engineering and metalwork firm made the vast majority of the braziers, goblets, candlesticks, swords, shields and metal implements that were used in the movie and the craftsmanship applied by him equalled the artistry employed by Corrib Crafts. No stone was left unturned to match the designs provided by the history buffs in order to best replicate artefacts from ninth century Wessex. Mr. Dooley has extremely positive memories of David Hemmings, one of the few who has.

"I liked Hemmings. He was a clever man, a very clever man, and I could always see that there was more to him than the silly playboy image portrayed of him. He was a good actor too, he had talent, and I respect people who have talent. We socialised with him a little bit, Robbie and myself (Robert Molloy, former T.D., Minister and Mayor of Galway) and got to know him quite well. He liked gambling and was always trying to organise people to get together and play. He had endless money to throw around, more than the rest of us and that's why he always won. I got eighty pounds up on him once and managed to leave the table with Robbie's help before he won it all back again... Hemmings showed great ability in being able to get that charity show on the road and it was an absolutely magnificent achievement. The success of it was mainly down to him, even though a lot more very fine people took part."

Mr Dooley didn't say it in so many words but I got the impression from talking to him that Hemmings was let down by the film, for whatever reason. Perhaps it was the cinematography that wasn't quite right (and he did remember that Hemmings was constantly hopping up during and after his scenes, looking though the camera viewfinder and checking the angles and asking questions, so he was thoroughly involved in the process. He didn't take his work lightly at all, according to Mr. Dooley, and was completely involved in his craft. *"He had an extremely strong technical interest in what was going on around him and that's another reason why I liked this guy. There was something other to him than that flamboyant foolish 22-year-old or whatever he was at the time."*

Clive Donner was also a man that Christy had great respect for and yet he felt that the director, for whatever reason, again, wasn't firing on all artistic cylinders for the film. He can't put a finger on it but no more than Tom Dowd in Tuam, Dooley couldn't understand, upon seeing the film, where on earth all of the things he'd made had disappeared. There was hardly any sign of them, apart from the obvious swords and shields.

Bobby Molloy, Christy Dooley and David Hemmings. *(Connacht Tribune* Files)

Prunella Ransome and Mary (Maisie) Dooley. *(Connacht Tribune* Files)

VIKING SUMMER

Dooley saw the movie in Leicester Square in London about a year later and and apart from wondering where all of his metal braziers and numerous other props had gone, his strongest memory is laughing at how ridiculous it was. *"It lacked verve, action and excitement. And it was much too long. It was like they were trying to make two different films at the same time, showing Alfred as an intellectual and then using him as a fighter on the battlefield. I told them that at the time, when we were designing the items they required, that the minute levels of detail would be wasted on screen. It was madness, all the work that went into it."* The final irony was that the eventual film didn't seem genuine even though every single item Dooley made for it was based on absolutely authentic designs and drawings from the British Museum. *"So much emphasis on precision, all wasted."* So, that's another possibility we can rule out as a a contributory factor to the failure of the film – it lacked nothing whatsoever in props authenticity. It seems, too, that Hemmings was 100% committed to excelling in his craft, however much of a social gadfly he may have been out of hours.

Apart from his metalwork on the movie, Christy Dooley (who is a well known jazzman in Galway city) is connected to Lord Killanin and Bobby Molloy in another context, that of swimming, more specifically via the 1972 Munich Olympics and Mark Spitz. Lord K was a member of the Olympic movement at that time and Dooley has been President of the Irish Amateur Swimming Association. In Munich he was a line judge on Mark Spitz's lane and although Michael Phelps bettered Spitz's thirty-six-year-old seven gold medal record during the 2008 Beijing Olympics, he was the hero of the moment in '72. On *Alfred The Great*, Dooley was also involved in a swimming capacity when the Viking longship was being moved from one side of the Corrib to the other, as the film makers were trying to frame Menlo Castle in the background of the shot.

A Great Goblet Hunt went on in the run-up to the making of the film in March 68, when the hype machine was cranked up as MGM sought high and low for the exact type of vessel needed as an important prop for Alfred. It was supplied, eventually, by Dooley's firm. The manufactured media tizzy made all of the papers, but separate from the hoopla, the actual goblet itself was quite an intricate piece of work. It was a replica jewel-studded medieval goblet, made by hand and eventually featured clearly in the movie when used by Hemmings to toast his various victories over the Danes.

Dooley doesn't know the whereabouts of the goblet but he does have two of the hundreds of

THE FILMING OF MGM'S 'ALFRED THE GREAT' IN GALWAY IN 1968

KING ALFRED GETS HIS CUP OF CHEER

Daily Mirror cutting, the headline celebrating the fact that a suitable goblet had been found for the King of Wessex, enabling 'Alf to get his cheer'.

VIKING SUMMER

> **An Irish goblet for Alfred the Great**
> *Express Staff Reporter*
>
> THE SEARCH for a film star's jewel-studded goblet has ended in a small wrought-iron foundry in Galway.
>
> The film company, M.G.M. wants the goblet for David Hemmings, who plays the lead in "Alfred the Great" to be filmed in Galway early this summer.
>
> The company wanted a single mock-up of the medieval gold goblets in the British museum so that Hemmings could toast his victories in mead.
>
> One of the few forges left that could make a hand-made reproduction of the goblet is owned by Galway businessman Christopher Dooley.
>
> Said 39-year-old Mr. Dooley: "There are very few craftsmen nowadays with sufficient skill to do this type of work. It will take one man a week to make it."

AN IRISH GOBLET FOR 'ALFRED'
Taken from the *Daily Express* of 28 March 1968. This cutting describes how the search by MGM for a jewel-studded goblet ended in a small wrought-iron foundry in Galway, belonging to Christy Dooley.

urns that were thrown for the film, designed in part by Ann Burke, a daughter of the stained-glass artist, Harry Clarke.

Shields in the film weighed 16 pounds and Hemmings (a slight man) had quite a job with them. He asked Christy to make them a little lighter so the work began to reduce their weight while retaining their dual function to both identify visually the particular chief and clan, and to make a recognisable *"clang"*, a noise that could be identified in the height of battle.

Explained Dooley: *"We made the base of very light gauge aluminium. We made the strips from hammered copper, and there was a lot of very intricate copper-wire work around the edges. It was embossed. I kept saying to the film people,"* (and he had many dealings with a woman from the film, a buyer called Biddy O'Kelly) *"that this detail was a waste but they kept saying go ahead. They were very particular about the standard of work that went into that film."* Christy's workshop was in Munster Avenue and he dealt a lot too with Patrick McLoughlin, Set Dresser, and Michael Stringer.

One of the more amusing incidents that Christy Dooley recalls concerns a visit he made in the company of some friends out to Castlehackett one day when Hemmings was filming the 'pool scene' on Knockma. Although the weather was great, the water itself was icy cold, filling up a large circular hole dug into the ground that can be seen quite near the beginning of the actual film. Hemmings kept hopping in and out of it, buck naked, as a lowly minion warmed it up for him with a kettle of boiling water that was being heated on a primus camping stove, just out of shot. *"Hardly Hollywood glamour,"* he laughed.

Henry Comerford knocked great sport out of his involvement in the film, even though it was exceptionally hard work keeping all of the legal balls in the air. *"It was grist to my mill,"* he said, *"having been involved in the theatre."* He had separate business dealings with some of the people from the movie, including helping Stringer, McLoughlin and Donner to purchase

FILMING MGM'S "ALFRED THE GREAT" IN GALWAY, IRELAND, WITH 1,500 EXTRAS ENTAILED PLAN OF GIANT SCOPE

MGM's spectacular motion picture, "Alfred the Great," features two major battles. But the preparation for these Dark Ages conflicts between Alfred's Saxon army and the invading Danes could hardly have equalled the detailed preparation for the staging of this epic story, filmed entirely on location in County Galway, Ireland.

An abbreviated list of props required for the six weeks of filming the battle sequences alone included : 4,000 arrows, 1,600 swords, 1,800 spears, 1,500 shields, 800 daggers, 300 clubs and axes, 200 saddles, 60 horses, 12 rubber dummies (to play dead)—and three skeletons.

Casualties among the enthusiastic Irish extras included bloody noses, sprains and gashes. To quote director Clive Donner, "The problem was not in getting them to put everything into the scenes, but getting them to *stop.*"

Up to 1,500 extras appeared in the battle scenes. Among them were students from University College, contracted for the length of the production, and 450 soldiers from the Republican Army's Western and Southern command who made up the hard core of the Viking forces. One doctor, four ambulancemen, six nurses and two ambulances were in attendance on locations all the time.

The costumes for the picture were made from hand-dyed material. Costume designer Jocelyn Rickards found this imperative in order to get the exact colors needed. Miss Rickards spent a week with her assistant dyeing rough fabrics in six 44-gallon drums. This entailed working on more than 27,000 yards of material.

The locations for "Alfred the Great" extended over three main sites of about 90 acres each. On one a complete studio was built for interior filming. For the others, 30 tents on each housed ancillary services—canteen, wardrobe, special effects and workshops. Drying-tents were provided for extras during wet weather. In all cases, bad weather was not permitted to hinder filming, even when roads turned into a morass of two-feet-deep mud.

All but one of the locations was within 20 miles of the crew's headquarters in Galway City. Even so, a fleet of 50 hired cars was required, with additional trucks and jeeps. More than 1,000 extras, plus 100 crew members, had to be transported each day to locations. Twenty-two school buses were hired from the local education authority and the army transported its men in 27 three-ton trucks.

At least 3,000 meals and snacks were served each day on location, six days per week. The Irish extras, like the English crew, preferred tea to coffee, and 200 gallons were made each day. About half that amount of coffee also disappeared daily down thirsty throats. Local ladies supplied 200 pounds of home-made cake a day, 150 loaves of bread and 2,500 rolls.

Most meals (except on Fridays) consisted of meat and potatoes. More than 600 pounds of prime Irish meats went through the kitchen each day, three tons of potatoes were peeled per week, and the crew alone got through 20 cases of fruit a day.

In Ireland's hottest summer for years, the Emerald Isle lost its legendary 40 shades of green, so six gardeners were employed full-time to spray the grass green.

Communications required some ingenuity. Five sets of walkie-talkies were used in the battle scenes, six loud-hailers and a vast amount of lungpower. Over 1,200 telephone calls a day were made by the unit, so special lines were installed by the department of Posts and Telegraphs.

All lighting and power came from independent sources. Fifteen lighting trucks supplied 15,000 amps, more than the daily requirements of the County Galway town of Oughterard (pop. 3,500).

Many of the props used in "Alfred the Great" were authentic relics, supplied from the collections of local antiquarians, and from the private collection of Lord Killanin, production associate to producer Bernard Smith.

Major construction feats, apart from the laying of a total of 12 miles of bedded roads, was the 300-ft. white horse, modeled on the ancient one in Berkshire. The horse was excavated to a depth of two feet and 25 tons of plaster were required to fill it. It will remain on the Castle Hackett location slopes, a mute but permanent reminder of MGM's aesthetic venture.

A Bernard Smith-James R. Webb production in Panavision and color, "Alfred the Great" stars David Hemmings, Michael York, Prunella Ransome and Colin Blakely. Ken Taylor and James R. Webb wrote the screenplay, based on a story by Webb.

This cutting lists, in exquisite detail, the ins and outs and magnificent logistical involvement, many of the requirements – physical and otherwise – that were needed to get the show on the road. It's one of the few places where Galway is mentioned as the main location for filming (we mustn't forget Killinure in Westmeath either, where segments of the movie were shot on the River Shannon), and illustrates that everything but the kitchen sink was thrown at the production.

There's a quote in it from director, Clive Donner, to the effect that "the problem was not in getting them to put everything into the scenes, but getting them to stop." Jocelyn Rickards, Costume Designer on *Alfred The Great,* and a woman who subsequently went on to marry Clive Donner after meeting him on set of that actual film, found it imperative to hand-dye the cloth needed for the picture, in order to get the precise colours required. Apparently she spent a week with her assistant dyeing rough fabrics in six 44-gallon drums, involving the use of some 27,000 yards of material.

All but one of the locations was within 20 miles of the crew's headquarters in Galway City but, even so, a fleet of 50 hired cars was required, plus additional trucks and Jeeps. More than 1,000 extras, plus 100 crew members, had to be transported daily to locations, requiring the hiring of twenty-two school buses from the local education authority. On top of that, a startling 27 three-ton trucks were needed to move the army personnel about. Heady stuff indeed and it's really no wonder that MGM was known locally as 'Money Gone Mad'.

VIKING SUMMER

Aerial photograph of the location at Killinure on the River Shannon where the opening scenes of the rampaging and pillaging in the film were shot (Courtesy of Sven Neuberg)

properties in Ireland. He knows full well that *Alfred* didn't do much for any of their careers. Donner never renovated the castle he bought on the Galway/Dublin road, Stringer had an interest in a place in Kinvara, and Patrick McLoughlin, the flamboyant set dresser from the picture, bought a house near Corrofin, Co. Clare, where he lived for some time with his elderly mother.

Apparently McLoughlin's nickname was *The Cardinal*, such was his enthusiasm for extraordinarily elegant apparel, and much good-humoured cheer greeted his positively regal arrival onto the top of Knockma each morning. Sarah Whiting, Michael Stringer's daughter, is still in touch with Mr. McLoughlin and a mention is made in her diary of 'Patrick's birthday party' whilst in Ireland in 1968.

Paul Stader, the stunt coordinator, was a person whom Comerford found fascinating, particularly because of his role of providing a 'fight' focus for the camera in the middle of many of the battle scenes. They didn't know it then, but we learned later that the production was completely undersupplied with stuntsmen for a movie that had such extravagant and sprawling battle scenes. Could this be the first hairline crack we see in the film's preparation? A little penny pinching that eventually sank the ship for a ha'pence worth of tar? Christy Dooley, too, spoke of what he perceived to have been an absence of discipline sometimes evident in the battle formations, lacking the singular precision that pertained in a movie

David Hemmings on horseback, Ross Lake 1968

like *Braveheart*. Stader had been a stuntsman in Johnny Weismuller's *Tarzan* films, but could he have been left dangling out on a limb in *Alfred*?

There's no gainsaying the fact that huge attention was lavished on detail, but was it properly focussed? Henry Comerford talks of the day he rambled out to Castlehackett to meet his client, the owner of Castlehackett. *"When I went out to meet Mr. Percy Paley, they were spraying the grass green because it had become worn from all the filming they were doing. As well as that, there were big wind machines, extraordinary things, in behind the bushes*

VIKING SUMMER

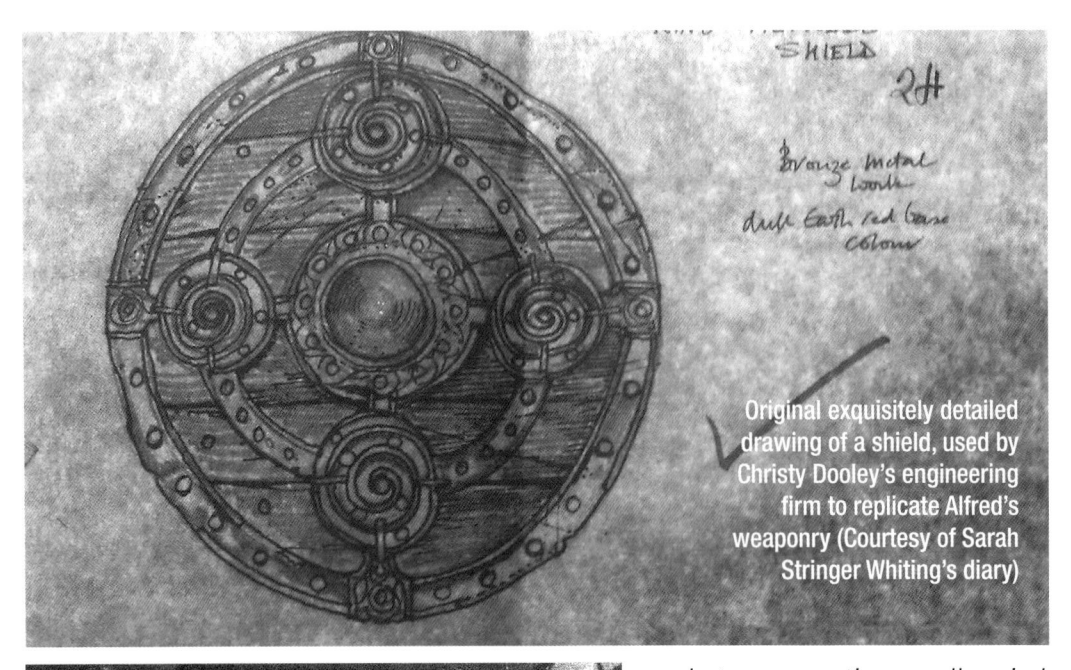

Original exquisitely detailed drawing of a shield, used by Christy Dooley's engineering firm to replicate Alfred's weaponry (Courtesy of Sarah Stringer Whiting's diary)

Photograph of shields published in *The Connacht Tribune* at the time

and trees creating, well, wind, obviously. It really was just extraordinary." And indeed it was, but was it the best possible use of the enormous skill-set available to the production, dyeing the grass green? Apparently Mr Paley was extremely glad to receive payment for the use of his property and his water spring, Tobermina, sweet well. Comerford had been involved in *The Rising of the Moon,* a trilogy shot in Galway 1956 and released in 1957. Parts of it were filmed around the Spanish Arch in the city and as a matter of some interest, the now 82-year-old jazz musician, Ronnie Burke, was also involved in that cinematic vehicle, as well as having played a role in *The Quiet Man.* Directed by Ford, whose directorial antics at the Spanish Arch were recalled by Comerford with some amusement, *The Rising* was produced by Lord Killanin and was presented by Warners. Henry C agreed that *Alfred The Great* wasn't too bad at all of a film and got an unusually bad press for some reason, but he was adamant that parts of it were daft.

The MGM liaison with whom Henry worked most closely during his stint with the picture was Hugh Harlow, named in our cast list as Unit Manager of the 1st Unit – there were two. Through pressure of time he had to meet with Henry at odd times and in odd places, including George McDonagh's thatched pub in Oranmore. It suited both men to meet there, it being a sort of a 'half-way house' smack bang in the middle of a junction that led on to Galway, Castlehackett, and Loughrea, Kilchreest, Shannon or Dublin.

The fight scenes, especially the Battle of White Horse Hill on Knockma, were extraordinary feats of cooperative cinematic choreography and to this day, it's dizzying to read the battle plan. Julian Senior, then a 30-year-old publicity guy working for MGM, in an article for the UK industry magazine, *Photoplay,* explained in some detail how to film a medieval battle. The preparations in Castlehackett began on May 13th 1968 and filming began on July 1st.

Senior describes the sun rising from the east onto the wooded valley, the silence suddenly giving way to the rhythmic insistent war cry that has terrified the Wessex peasants ever since Danish incursions began on English soil. "AN-TAN-AN-TAN, AN-TAN-AN-TAN" comes the eerie chant from the mist and when it rises, row upon row of fearsome bearded Norsemen appear, clad in silver breastplates, spears held ready. Spearheading the advance are three men, one of them being Guthrum (Michael York), who approach remorselessly down the valley towards the smouldering torches that outline Alfred's camp.

Charlotte and David Stringer, on location at the site of King Alfred's hut, Ross Lake

VIKING SUMMER

Frank Deacy, as 'Fr. Joe' in *Love and Savagery,* Ballyvaughan, 2008 (Mary J. Murphy)

That's another vivid memory Chick Gillen (retired Galway barber and former Seapoint Ballroom doorman) has, the smell of smoke that came off all involved in the filming, including the highly paid movie stars, because there was usually a fire going somewhere, whether in the heat of battle or just for cooking, as well as the torches that were burning all over the place for the night scenes. Senior continues, saying that just when it seems that Alfred's camp is bound to be overrun, the ram's horn trumpet sounds from the bottom of the valley where the Saxons are encamped and the hill comes to life as the men of Wessex sweep down on top of the Danes, catching them by surprise, fighting like men possessed. Bloody bodies tumble all sides as the Vikings attempt to regroup, the Saxons howl victoriously amidst the terrible slaughter and the hundreds, perhaps thousands of men, remain locked in combat on the hill slopes.

For a while, Alfred stays on the edge of the battle, but his warrior side eventually outweighs his priestly side, after which he leaps into the midst of the murderous melee and begins to defend himself against the random blows that rain down upon his head. That's the kind of frantic melodrama that Smith and Donner were after, as they devised the film, and if you actually look at the movie, those battle scenes are marvellously exciting and are pulled off spectacularly well. The invading Viking chants are silenced and when the sun finally rises the ground is strewn with the wounded, the dead and the dying and one can hardly imagine that such slaughter in the real Battle of White Horse Hill lasted barely 40 minutes. It's pure 'Boy's

Frank Deacy, as an extra in *'Alfred The Great'* at Ross Lake in 1968

Own' stuff and a far cry from the deceptively gentle opening scene, reminiscent of the pastoral early shots in *The Quiet Man,* when the shepherd boy (Robin Asquith) and the shepherdess (Margaret Taylor) cavort around some standing stones just before the Danes land, plunder and pillage. (Those standing 'stones', as we know now, were papier mâché props, made in timber frames from paper and daub). Those scenes were filmed at Killinure on the River Shannon.

There's great reportage of the night-filming at Knockma on page 2 of *The Tuam Herald* from

VIKING SUMMER

Filming, Ross Lake 1968

20 July 1968, where Martin Tyrrell described the cinematic happenings. The entrance to the film set was guarded by a corporal from the Irish army and the logistics of the equipment on site were such that within 500 yards from the gate there were thirty-six caravan tents, more than fifty trucks and Jeeps, four ambulances, three canteens, eight caravans and dozens of bright lights. Eight powerful arc lights surrounded an area of some two acres and extras and participants were milling all over the place, preparing for the shooting that was soon to commence. A Miss Ita Murphy from Headford was mentioned, she being particularly delighted to have shaken hands with David Hemmings, who spoke apparently of his plans to

Filming, Ross Lake 1968

visit Ireland often in the future. He was drinking tea, we're told, as was Miss Ransome. Clive Donner, the director, took up his perch beside the main camera that was partially shaded by a huge umbrella, as the adventure was about to begin. *"Action!"*

The *Herald* article went on to explain how Donner had travelled around extensively before opting to film in the west of Ireland, and told of Lord Killanin's delight upon discovering the suitability of Knockma as a location. Julian Senior was on hand to elaborate on the history of Alfred and the 9th century, and described how silence fell on set as the director's voice

VIKING SUMMER

called for quiet; filming to start in one minute. Nobody, perhaps not even their own mothers, would have recognised the locals who took part as extras, they being heavily disguised in beards and flowing locks, and some of whom included Tommy Dooley, Paddy Joe Monaghan, Fintan Donoghue and Mick Fahey.

One of the more overlooked aspects about the making of that film in County Galway in that summer of '68 was the fact that many university students weren't forced to go away to take summer jobs.

There's a great flavour of the time captured in an email we got from Newfoundland, Canada, from Frank Deacy, who was born and raised in Galway, went to 'the Bish', left UCG in 1968, taught in Presentation College, Bray, for two years before settling in Newfoundland since 1971.

He became aware of our trawl via a note placed in Tom Kenny's *'Old Galway'* section in the *Galway Advertiser*, and explained that his dealings with *Alfred* came about when he joined the merry bunch of hundreds of other University College Galway students who stayed home that summer, keeping the tills of Galway buzzing with MGM cash.

The level of detail in Deacy's communication is fantastic and can be used as a template to describe what a typical day would have been like for a UCG student extra in battle. After hopping on the MGM buses at the Spanish Arch in Galway at 6.30am, they arrived on set, reported to wardrobe (Jocelyn Rickards' domain) and were outfitted with itchy, scratchy clobber, including a wig. Everything was checked back in against their names each evening. The craic was mighty but the days were long and tiring, often consisting of a 12-hour stretch. Tea breaks, lunch breaks and evening breaks chopped up the day and were an opportunity for the students and soldiers, who loathed each other, to glare with deeply satisfying mutual contempt. The slagging on all sides was relentless and sporadic bouts of action were separated by hours of tedium as the director waited for clouds and the dark, dank drizzle required for the purpose of cinematic realism. The students played cards ad nauseam, sunbathed (a novelty for many) or snoozed away the day, snuggled into the cosy round bulge indented into their shields.

When they filmed the famous 'Phalanx' battle scene near Ross Lake in Moycullen, Deacy said that the activity got semi-serious at times and there were a lot of richocheting swords

Prunella Ransome (centre) and her handmaiden, Sinéad Cusack, leave the court of Wessex as hostages of the Vikings. Still from the movie (copyright MGM).

VIKING SUMMER

David Hemmings and Jane Fonda in *Barbarella*, 1968

Hugh Harlow and his wife

The author with Peter Price at Knockma in May 2008

The Filming of MGM's 'Alfred The Great' in Galway in 1968

A tapestry from the church scenes in the movie, made by the Carmelite nuns, Loughrea, property of Christy Dooley

Joseph Cunningham (RIP), Feeragh, Beclare. An extra in *Alfred The Great* during the long hot summer of 1968

An urn from the film, property of Christy Dooley, and thrown originally by Ann Burke, daughter of stained-glass artist, Harry Clarke

VIKING SUMMER

Above: Tobermina track up the north (front) of Knockma, leading to the White Horse

Below: Mattie Glynn, Bridie Dowd, Mary Glynn, Mary Flanagan (RIP) and Mick Glynn, all of whom have fond memories of the filming of *Alfred The Great*.

Love comes to the scholarly prince Alfred when he is reunited with his childhood sweetheart, Aelhswith of Mercia. Still from the movie (copyright MGM)

VIKING SUMMER

Joe Flanagan,
Cave, Caherlistrane
Joe was involved in *Alfred The Great* as an extra during filming at Castlehackett. His neighbour, Leo Courtney of Pollnahallia, clearly recalls the day that Joe called to his house one hot summer day with long hair, a wild beard and a smoke-covered face.
(photo © Cait Cummins)

Charlie and Annie Coen, Corandrum, Claregalway
Charlie had a high-speed hair-raising encounter with an MGM employee at 3a.m. one night during filming in the summer of 1968. Following a puncture in the dead of night, Charlie was picked up by this unknown movie Samaritan (who drove a Ford Thunderbird at extraordinary speeds) and was whisked to Galway from Claretuam, through crowds of people who were making their way on foot into the market in Galway city later that day. {photo courtesy of Margaret (Coen) Hanley}

Alfred The Great wood carving in Corrib Crafts, 2007
(© Mary J. Murphy)

The Filming of MGM's 'Alfred The Great' in Galway in 1968

Kilchreest Castle 2008. Note the crumbling battlements at the top left that were squared-off and perfected for the film

Castle Hackett Tower, Belclare (1995, © Mary J. Murphy)

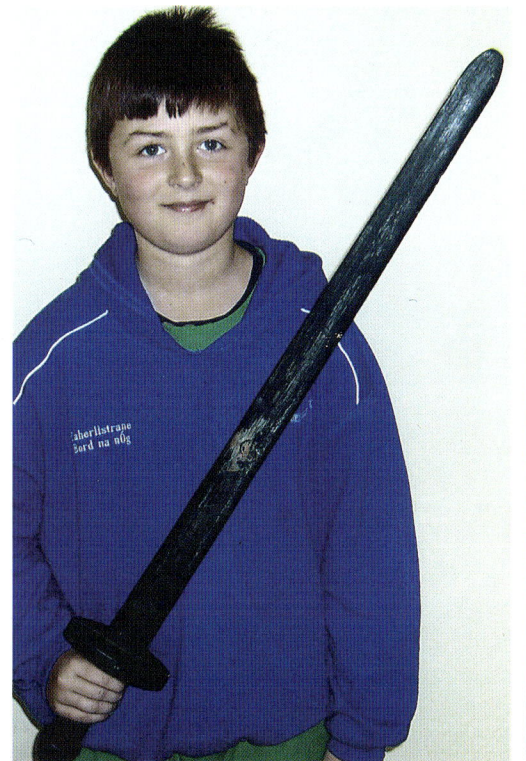

Morgan Glynn holding a sword used in the movie, property of Patrick Stewart

Oranmore Castle, in which David Hemmings lived during filming

VIKING SUMMER

Al O'Dea and Corrib Crafts montage (© Mary J. Murphy)

Joe Muldoon (RIP), Ballintleva, who was an extra in *Alfred the Great*, with his wife Mary

Willie and Mary Cunningham, Biggera, Belclare
Willie worked on location when filming took place at Castlehackett, using a tractor and trailer that were often employed to move camera rostrums from one point to another. The agricultural machine he purchased afterwards was forever known as 'Alfred's hay-turner'. Mr. Cunningham is now in his 91st year. (photo courtesy of M. Cunningham)

At 22 years of age, Prince Alfred gained a throne and saved a kingdom. Still from the movie (copyright MGM)

King Alfred (David Hemmings) prepares to lead his Saxon army into battle against the Danish Vikings. Still from the movie (copyright MGM)

Painting from the film by Michael Stringer, given to us by Layne Stringer

Paintings from the film by Michael Stringer, given to us by Layne Stringer

Painting from the film by Michael Stringer, given to us by Layne Stringer

Painting from the film by Michael Stringer, given to us by Layne Stringer

The Filming of MGM's 'Alfred The Great' in Galway in 1968

Top: All of Corrib Crafts – Al O'Dea sitting at the front with: At back left to right: Charley Lynch, Tom Dowd and John Daly.

Left: Tom Dowd of Corrib Crafts in his workshop.

Above: Cover of Anvil Publishing's *The Quiet Man,* written by Maurice Walsh in 1935 and filmed in 1951 by John Ford, with Lord Killanin as Assoc. Producer

Peter Price with Edward G. Robinson. This photograph shows Peter Price on the left – who was Assistant Director on *Alfred The Great* – in an earlier movie, *Sammy Going South,* with the major motion picture star, Edward G. Robinson. Price has worked within the film industry since 1949 and amongst many other films, he has been involved in *The System,* Michael Winner's first feature film, with Oliver Reed; *Chato's Land* with Charles Bronson; *Shalako* with Brigitte Bardot and Sean Connery, plus many, many others

Lough Hackett (New Year's Eve 2007, © Mary J. Murphy)

Pictured left to right: Tony Spratling (camera operator), Alex Thomson (director of cinematography), David Hemmings and Peter Price – with Clive Donner looking down from the back at extreme right (photo given to us by Peter Price)

Clive Donner at Killinure directing Margaret Taylor on papier mâché 'rocks', immediately prior to the invasion of the rampaging Vikings. Peter Price at extreme left with hands on head, and Alex Thomson in foreground (photo given to us by Peter Price)

VIKING SUMMER

and spears flying around, as well as tempers. *"When we had finished firing our spears, we then arrived to fight them in hand-to-hand style, but they had to stay in formation, both standing and kneeling, and we had to do the smacking with our swords. Of course they got hit and got really upset and some rackets started up. This only reinforced the usual soldier versus student scene at the time, but then the management solved this problem with a 'brainwave'. They employed extra soldiers, from I believe Athlone barracks, so it would be a case of soldier versus soldier, not versus student."* Apparently the Athlone soldiers disliked the Galway soldiers even more than both of them hated students !

In one shot, Deacy and his buddies were caught resting where they shouldn't have been and were hauled into a running scene with Hemmings as a 'punishment'. Not the most popular of leading men *("he was stuck up")*, the plan was they had to chase Hemmings, who proclaimed himself quite fit. He was not to know that Deacy and his buddies were fitter – two rugby players and a track athlete – and they left him for dead when filming began. To the utter consternation of director, Clive Donner, the scene had to be done umpteen times as the onlooking students hooted and hollered from the sidelines.

Some students kept up an ongoing summer-long battle of wits with MGM, constantly trying to outfox their payment system. The sheer difficulty of keeping track of the flux and flow of hundreds of wily students, some there full-time, some part-time and some used only on a daily basis, assisted their devious manipulations. 'Wet pay' was agitated for when they were fiming at Ross Lake, some got away with being paid twice for the same week's work by queueing up a second time after changing their clothes, some disappeared off to Galway for the week entirely and only returned on Friday for their cash, and yet others got a thing called *'waiting money'.* That, explained Deacy, was payment for queueing for hours in the blistering sun, waiting for their cash. *"Only in Galway could that happen!"* he said.

Founder and first editor of the immensely successful *Galway Advertiser* newspaper, Ronnie O'Gorman was another of the UCG students who took part in *Alfred The Great*. *"I played a dead warrior and lay in the fields of Collinamuck (at Ross Lake) for hours. Amazingly, I was paid £7 a day and I remember I bought a portable record player (for such they were known in those days!) and was very pleased with myself. I was in London at the time and went to it when it opened."* He added that it was a ghastly film, savaged by the critics and didn't bring him any fame or fortune either because *"sad to say my dying and death scene was cut!"*

Filming battle scenes at Ross Lake 1968

Oliver Muldoon now lives in Cape Cod, Massachusetts, but participated as a student extra for 4 days *"some place near Tuam"*, (Castlehackett), and has strong recall of early rising in the morning and very long arduous days. *"As I was doing a UCG exam that fall I had to bow out in favour of less onerous duties as a piano player at the old Foster Park Hotel in Salthill."*

The one highlight that has stuck in his mind concerns the day when one of *"the suits"* (MGM people) *"got very steamed... after they'd spent hours setting up an ambush scene. We came charging down the hill in a blood-curdling onslaught onto the troops below. They had a*

VIKING SUMMER

Filming battle scenes at Ross Lake 1968

camera set up near where I was passing and some fella went right in front of it without blinking an eye, and his black horn-rimmed glasses totally spoiled the scene. Someone shouted 'Cut!' and we were ordered back up the hill."

Aidan Walsh, now in the pharmacy business, was another student extra, and so too was Brendan Forkan, then a medical student. His recall is of trying to convince the people at his interview in Tuam that he was well able to ride a horse. The pay was better if you could bring an extra dimension to the performance, and horsemanship was one of those added-extras. Forkan spent numerous nights out in Castlehackett as a Saxon dressed up to the nines in medieval stuff, and brandishing plastic swords. *"We ran down the hill and attacked the soldiers."* he said, *"and it was important to get to know a soldier, for fighting purposes, so no one would get hurt. We were fed on site and got paid at the end of each night. It seemed to be a fortune at the time."* Back then, he said, a return ticket from Tuam to London was less than £5.

Joe Varley (who lives in Malahide, County Dublin with his wife, Dorothy) has a particularly vivid memory of the long hard cold hours spent on the top of Knockma. They were told when they signed up that they would be spending most of July at Castlehackett, so were prepared for a long haul.

"The Friday before we moved out to Castlehackett, we spent the afternoon on the drill field at Renmore Barracks where we were instructed in sword fighting by members of the British Olympic fencing team. On the Monday or the Tuesday that we went out to Castlehackett, pick-up time was at 5pm in the Spanish Arch area and we would have got out to the set at about 6.30pm. They filmed in the valley, a good three or four fields up from the main road." That's near the Tobermina track, the name translating from the Irish to *"sweet well"*, Percy Paley's water supply. *"In the field just off that road they had the costume tent, catering tent and all the technical and other facilities. The permanent extras were assigned as Saxons for the battle, the Danes being soldiers from Galway, Athlone and Cork. They wanted to convey the idea of the disciplined Danes as against Saxon rabble."* And that, right there, is more excellent MGM forward planning.

Varley continued: *"As well as ourselves and the soldiers there was a large number of temporary extras who were mainly from Tuam and Headford."* He feels that on the night there were *"at least 1,000 people on the set between actors, production and extras."* Varley, who signed up for his tenure on ATG at Woodquay in Galway, explains what the plan was for the night's battle filming.

"They had three major camera systems set up – one at the top of the valley to cover the Danes, one at the right-hand side to cover the Saxons and the other was at the tents at the base of the valley where they were doing 'interiors' at the start of the night, the sequence where Alfred's brother gave him command of the army, as his leg was broken. It was a very fine July night and we had been costumed, given our weapons, and been fed by

VIKING SUMMER

Photograph taken at Castlehackett, given to us by Peter Price. Note Patrick McLoughlin's (Set Dresser and nominated for an Oscar award for his work on *Becket* and *Anne of A Thousand Days)* magnificent Rolls-Royce in the background, to the left of the tractor, and Clive Donner's name on his rather modest director's chair, to the right of the bin. Peter Price is sitting aloft with a megaphone and behind him are Joe Knowles (clipboard), Alex Thomson, Jimmy Devis and K.C. Jones. On camera is Harvey Harkin and under the camera stands Cyril Swerne

about 9 o'clock. Our position then," said Joe Varley, "was at the right side of the valley, looking down, and I would think we got up there about 10 o'clock. It was quite bright and the second assistant director, who was in charge of us, told us what was going to happen. They had us in position there while it was still light and we would have to stay there until dawn because they wanted to use that half-light of dawn to film the attack on the Danish army coming down the valley. The food would be brought up to us about 2.30 in the morning."

Joe Varley explained that there was a slight difference in outlook and attitude towards the filming process

Left: Peter Price on "his lovely ass" at Castlehackett

between the experienced permanent extras like himself and the temps, who were brought in on a "needs be" basis. The guys, like Joe, who had been with the film for about five weeks by the time Castlehackett hill came around, were prepared to persevere through the huge slots of boredom and ennui that are part and parcel of the game of filming. Mad spurts of action interspersed with bouts of endless time-wasting were what they'd spent nearly six weeks at so they weren't quite as antsy or impatient as the local temporary extras who were just called in for the battles.

"Things," said Varley, *"were going hot and heavy between the 'temporaries' and the 2nd assistant director who was very English and very insistent. However, the arrival of food and the tea, which was very warm and sweet, seemed to calm everyone down. It was a very interesting night although it got very cold at about three o'clock in the morning. In our group we had stuntmen and special effects people who explained to us exactly what was going to happen – there was to be a hand-to-hand combat between a Danish and a Saxon stuntman, a designated fighting area and a small camera crew to film the part where a Danish horseman was to get an arrow in the back. From about 5am onwards, the 'lights' people called the shots. The shooting 'window of opportunity' was not long enough but from about 6 a.m. on things started to happen. They had a system of walkie-talkies and in about an hour, they got got the Danish advance ("AN-TAN! AN-TAN! AN-TAN!") down the valley and the start of the Saxon attack. I am quite familiar with the film and I think this part is visually very attractive and was worth all the effort that went into it. We were back at costumes and weapons by 8 a.m. and I am not sure if we got a full breakfast or sandwiches for the bus but everybody was really tired at this stage and just wanted to get home, back into Galway. However, we got paid eight old pounds for the night which was great money in 1968."*

Varley described Clive Donner as *"Mister Big"*, who had come with a huge reputation on the heels of the immense success of his previous film, *Here We Go Round the Mulberry Bush*, a satire on 60s London. *"He always seemed preoccupied or under pressure... and we would have seen him working a lot on interiors, particularly the wedding scene, the Danish banquet scene and the Saxon flogging, which were all done in Kilchreest in June. He always went to five or six takes and I seem to remember him going to 10 or 11 takes (sometimes) with everybody well fed up at the end."* Peter Price, listed in our MGM personnel pages as First Assistant Director in the 1st Unit – there were two – was described by Joe Varley as a man *"who was very good at managing big crowds and very pleasant to work with."* He feels

VIKING SUMMER

Members of the Defence Forces (from the Barracks in Renmore) rehearsing at Castlehackett (photograph courtesy of Captain Kevin McDonald)

that he was *"the big boss"* at the battlefields too and recalls that he was instrumental in the scene where Hemmings lets a big wolfhound loose, to chase after Ransome, who's wearing a 'modern,' 60s wide-brimmed sun hat.

Joe Varley remembers another occasion, on the August Bank Holiday Monday at Kilchreest, when Donner wanted additional footage for the opening scene on the Shannon. Varley was dressed as a Dane that day and recalls himself and four or five guys dragging stunned sheep up through a field. Brian Cooke (listed as 2nd Assistant Director, also in the 1st Unit) was said by some to be awkward to work with at times, unlike one of his counterparts, Michael Stevenson - another 2nd Assistant Director on the same Unit. He got Varley's vote for being *"really brilliant. A really nice guy, very clear in his instructions, a great communicator, who kept you fully informed, important in film making, for they're chopping and changing all the time. He had worked with David Lean on* Lawrence of Arabia *in the Jordanian desert and was really good on the crowd scenes, particularly at Ross Lake, where they used a lot of older people."*

Of Redmond Morris he recalls that the son of Lord Killanin was a trainee director, working

**Members of the Defence Forces (from the Barracks in Renmore), as extras in *Alfred The Great*
(photograph given to us by Captain Kevin McDonald)**

mainly on the second unit, and also helped out on the battlefields. He found him pleasant but – obviously, at his age – inexperienced in comparison with some of the aforementioned. The chief cameraman, Alex Thomson, was one Varley never had any direct contact with but from his observations thought to be a fine professional who worked hand-in-glove with the lighting experts all the time.

The people Varley got to know best on the production were the young technicians, many of them from the Elstree area in north-east London who had gone to work in the studios there at 14 or 15 as either general operatives or in trades like electricians or carpenters. It was difficult for some of them as they were married and had small kids. On that August weekend, however, they chartered a plane from Shannon to London to get home to see their families. The points of contact for the UCG students and the MGM crew was age – most in their early to mid 20s – and soccer, playing a huge amount of it during the interminable hanging around that was part of the whole process. *"Indeed some of us, being members of UCG's soccer club, were able to get to the Grammar School at College Road and take part in a match, versus the MGM team, that August."*

VIKING SUMMER

Thomas Hodson, then a young lieutenant on detachment from the 12th Battalion, Clonmel, was involved in archery on the picture and recalls the input of Sergeant Michael Ryan. Explained Hodson:

"The director of the film or his historical advisers believed that there was evidence that Alfred's army was able, at a given signal, to deploy from a passive formation into an attacking formation, which won it many battles. They attempted, with no success over several days on Castlehackett Hill, to recreate this change of formation with a motley crew of soldiers and students."

Hodson continued: *"Mick Ryan, a superb NCO who had been my Platoon Sergeant the year before on a UN mission to Cyprus, put it to the director (Donner) that he would be able to organise a drill movement to accomplish this manoeuvre. He was given the opportunity to try out his plan. A bit shaky at the start but after a few attempts, all of Alfred's army, soldiers and students alike, followed Mick's directions given through a loud-hailer and performed to the director's satisfaction."* Hodson explained that *"the same group of soldiers from Clonmel were also involved in the making of Kubrick's* Barry Lyndon *almost ten years later."*

He told of how, after Ryan O'Neal (the star of *Barry Lyndon* and then hugely famous for his role in *Love Story*) had fluffed his lines for the umpteenth time whilst on horseback, an anonymous soldier was heard to shout, *'Ah, get the f***ing horse to say it!'*

Now a professor in the Department of English and Chair of the Board of the Centre for Irish Studies at the National University of Ireland, Galway, Professor Tadhg Foley was another UCG student, and grew his very first beard for *Alfred The Great*. He retains an MGM publicity still from the movie to this day, as well as a brooch, a keepsake from the time when he was a Mercian nobleman in the film, along with his friend, Jim Grealy.

We can deduce from the clarity of the recall of those extras, itemising all of the actions they had to undertake over weeks of filming, that superb planning and organising went into the setting up and choreography of the movie. There was nothing slipshod about the efforts that went into making the whole thing as 'real' as possible. All concerned might have been a lot better off and the film might have been eminently more watchable had they faked it a little more and not strained so much for authenticity. That yearning for precise ninth

Michael York on horseback at Ross Lake 1968

century replication appears to have drained the va-va-va voom, the life-force, from the project and may well have been one of the contributing causes of its failure. Castlehackett was a fabulous location for umpteen scenes, but what of Kilchreest? Was it an ill-chosen fly in the ointment?

Planning permission for the MGM studio at Eskershanone, Kilchreest, 1967, given to us by Sean Stewart, on whose family land the complex was built

KILCHREEST, COUNTY GALWAY
Location of MGM's studio complex during the filming of *Alfred The Great* in 1968 and of the then Jack Glynn's public house

CHAPTER FIVE

At Kilchreest, MGM took over an extensive area surrounding Patrick Stewart's home, using some 50 acres, following Lord K's surprise appearance one winter's day in 1967, as he clutched with him the outline of his modest proposal.

Mrs. Stewart remembers that film personnel called twice that day, and their daughter (Maura), barely out of her toddling years, recalls the flapdoodle that ensued when the helicopter clattered down to a halt in their farmyard. Once the parties had reached their agreement, planning permission for the studio complex appeared in the local *Connacht Tribune* newspaper shortly afterwards.

When we visited the Stewarts on St. Patrick's Day, 2008, forty years later, they were still able to work up a happy chuckle about the day Killanin arrived on their premises. One of the fields required by the film was covered in rocks back then, but Lord K said that it was perfect as there wasn't a house to be seen for miles. Mr. Stewart pointed to his back kitchen window,

VIKING SUMMER

towards Loughrea to the east, and explained that that's where much of the activity took part. The studio and the 1,000 year old Saxon villages were erected as you swing over towards the north, north-east from the house, and although they can't remember all of the names after four decades, they do remember that of Phil Topliss. He was the Construction Manager and they retain extremely pleasant memories of him. There was just one pole that spoiled the entire vista so MGM camouflaged it with branches and left it alone. Strangely enough, more than a year later ('69), when Paddy's brother in Australia saw the film, he didn't recognise a single person in it but he did spot a trio of trees that we saw ourselves, still standing tall and proud, out the back window of the Stewart home in March 2008.

"They wanted to knock them, too," said Mrs Stewart, *"but Paddy wouldn't let them go near them."* *"Between one thing and another,"* said Paddy, *"they were around the place for nearly two years. Phil Topliss was here at the very beginning and he was the last man we saw at the end, too."*

Of course the shock of the initial written communication shook them to the core – *"We didn't know what to make of it at all, and didn't reply for a while,"* said Mrs S. *"It was so out of the blue, who'd expect something like that to happen?"*

The construction of the complex, under the watchful eye of Topliss, lasted for six months and gave good employment to many local men. Prior to planning application, the existing purpose of the land was grazing and the proposed development was to include workshops, studios, offices, canteen, kitchen, toilets and exterior sets. The floor area of the proposed development was 26,250sq yards. Half of that was interior and the other half was constructed of temporary sets built on a huge poured concrete surface. As well as that yard area, lots of small concrete runs had to be poured, to be used as tracks for the cameras. Paddy Stewart remembers that the cost of the concrete for that surface was an astonishing £12,000 sterling, and the sewerage works – carried out by Burke and Clancy – added up to a further £14,000. *"The first thing MGM did,"* said Paddy S, *"was to build a Dutch haybarn with four bays (aisles) and that was for a workshop."* The production team also built a false top onto the local castle, topping it off with a huge flag.

Some of the filming near Stewart's was done at the huge old gates that form the entrance to the home of Lady Gregory at the Persse estate, but mostly it happened right outside their kitchen window in the big field on the Loughrea side that faced to the east. It was great fun

METRO-GOLDWYN-MAYER BRITISH STUDIOS LTD., Boreham Wood, Herts, England.

Please reply to:

The Lord Killanin,
30 Lansdown Road,
Dublin, 4.

Peter Stewart, Esq.,
Roxburgh,
Kilchreest,
Co. Galway.

Telephone: 63362   17th October, 1967

Dear Mr. Stewart,

I am Production Associate on the forthcoming picture ALFRED THE GREAT which it is hoped to make in Galway. One of the facilities we are looking for is an area in which to erect a temporary complex which would include facilities for shooting in bad weather. It is difficult to explain this on paper and I plan to visit you with the Art Director or representatives of the film in the not too distant future if you are agreeable in principle. My request is to rent from you the field on the Loughrea side of the road at Roxburgh for the erection of temporary structures. Naturally any structures not required by you afterwards would be removed. I understand that some of the land adjoining your field is the property of a Mr. Vincent Haley but I will not write to him until I hear from you that you would be agreeable to this in principle. We could then visit you to discuss rent, etc.

Yours sincerely,

Killanin

Lord Killanin's letter to Patrick Stewart, Kilchreest, in October 1967, seeking permission to use his land to make a film, an action which led to the erection of a 24,000 square foot (12,000ft uncovered) state-of-the-art studio on his farm

Directors: ROBERT H. O'BRIEN (Chairman – U.S.A.) · ARVID L. GRIFFEN (Managing Dir. – U.S.A.) · R. B. HUGHES · JACK KING · PAUL MILLS
Telephone: ELStree 2000 (20 lines) 01-953-2000   Telegrams: METROBRIT, BOREHAM WOOD   Telex 22502

VIKING SUMMER

at the time but Mrs Stewart was raising a family and there were days when they couldn't get in or out of their own house. *"There would be 700 or 800 men lying right out there some times,"* she smiled, *"and all of their trucks, lorries, Jeeps, vans, seven or eight buses from Galway bringing the extras in and out, ambulances (two on standby at all times) and nurses on standby, as well and fire engines on alert."*

Names of locals they recall being involved include Joe Callanan's mother, Joe McNamara, Gerry Connolly (the driver who brought Clive Donner around), Donal Raftery (also a taxi man from Craughwell), John Cunningham from Kilchreest, Christy Pender, Paddy Cooley and a Niland man and on the list goes. The Stewarts remember the chef on site, Festy Conlon, very well - *"He played a beautiful tin whistle,"* said Paddy, *"and he used to come up to the house here every night looking for home-made brown bread."* The statistics involved in the film production, both up at Stewart's in Eskershanore and at the other locations, are amazing. 600 pounds of meat were consumed daily (except Fridays), 3 tons of potatoes peeled, 20 cases of fresh fruit and 200 gallons of tea – with just half that amount of coffee swallowed every 24 hours. Some 27,000 yards of material were dyed in six 44-gallon drums by Jocelyn Rickards, Costume Designer, for uniforms; three main sites covered some 90 acres each in total; 30 tents housed canteens, special effects, wardrobes and workshops; 50 hired cars, trucks and Jeeps moved 100 crew – plus 1,000 extras – daily and the army moved around in 27 three-ton trucks. Six gardeners were employed full-time to keep the grass sprayed green and fresh; 1,200 'phone calls were made by the MGM crew daily; Posts and Telegraphs (the telephone company) cooperated by putting in lots of poles; lighting and power was made available independently by 15 trucks that supplied 15,000 amps – the same amount of power as required by the town of Oughterard, population 3,500. Twelve miles of bedded roads were made altogether in every location and 25 tons of plaster filled in the White Horse (200 ft long) on Castlehackett Hill. It's the logistics of setting up a small town, from scratch.

Water for the studio complex was to be sourced from the nearby stream, Owenshee (Lady Gregory's river), and was to be filtered and chlorinated before use. That planning application was dated 31 October 1967, the notice appeared in *The Connacht Tribune* on 3 November that same year and permission was granted on 1 December 1967, signed by C.A. Warner, County Engineer, on behalf of Galway County Council.

Paddy Stewart and his son Sean (who wasn't born when the film was made) showed us one of the swords that was used in the picture and MGM's own publicity material at the time explained just how many swords and weapons of war were used as props - 4,000 arrows; 1,600 swords; 1,800 spears; 1,500 shields; 800 daggers; 300 clubs and axes; 200 saddles; 60 horses (don't ask me to explain the 140 extra saddles – I can't); 12 rubber dummies (to play dead) and 3 skeletons. On top of that add up to 1,500 extras in the main battle sequences and 450 soldiers from the Western and Southern Command and we begin to get a clearer picture of the logistics involved. Those aspects of the movie appear to have been extremely well considered, so we can hardly lay the blame for the failure of *Alfred The Great* at the door of poor prop supply or shoddy materials either.

The Stewarts spoke of the large, excitable crowds that thronged around their house, coming out from Galway city and beyond, to witness filming when action sequences were underway. Locals participants they mentioned include Mrs. Madge Callanan and her daughter, Mary Murphy. Madge was one of the few female extras, and bought tiles for the kitchen floor from her movie earnings. Mary herself recalls the ten shillings they were offered as children for live frogs and crows. Eamon McNally of Barrack Street in Loughrea was an extra from the area, a Dane, and Michael Coy from Ballacurra, Kilchreest, recalled the day Prunella Ransome chased some local lads away from her red sports car, eventually ending up in Jack Glynn's yard which housed empty coffins among other things. Joe Callanan was heavily involved in the production, with the livestock, along with Joe McNamara. He was only about 17 and remembers the wild mountainy goats they had in pens that came all the way up from the Burren in County Clare, and spins in Michael York's green Mercedes, and York going out riding with them in a string of horses early in the morning, and Hemmings being a bit aloof, and Joe himself being paid £12 a day – big money then when he was on call.

In one famous scene that was shot at Knockma, Callanan remembers Colin Blakely riding a borrowed donkey for a scene and when the animal buckled under his weight the local farmer who owned him became agitated and started yelling, *"Me Ass! Me Ass! Ye've ruined me lovely ass!"*

Ned Waldron from Athenry worked with the ESB on site at the MGM studio at Eskershanore in Kilchreest and his recall illustrates, one more time, the great pains that were taken to ensure that all preparations were carried out to the highest standards. He worked under the direction of the Chief Engineer, Ken Krack, and was on the premises from late 1967 onwards, during a foot-and-mouth outbreak. A lot of local men worked there, in the initial

VIKING SUMMER

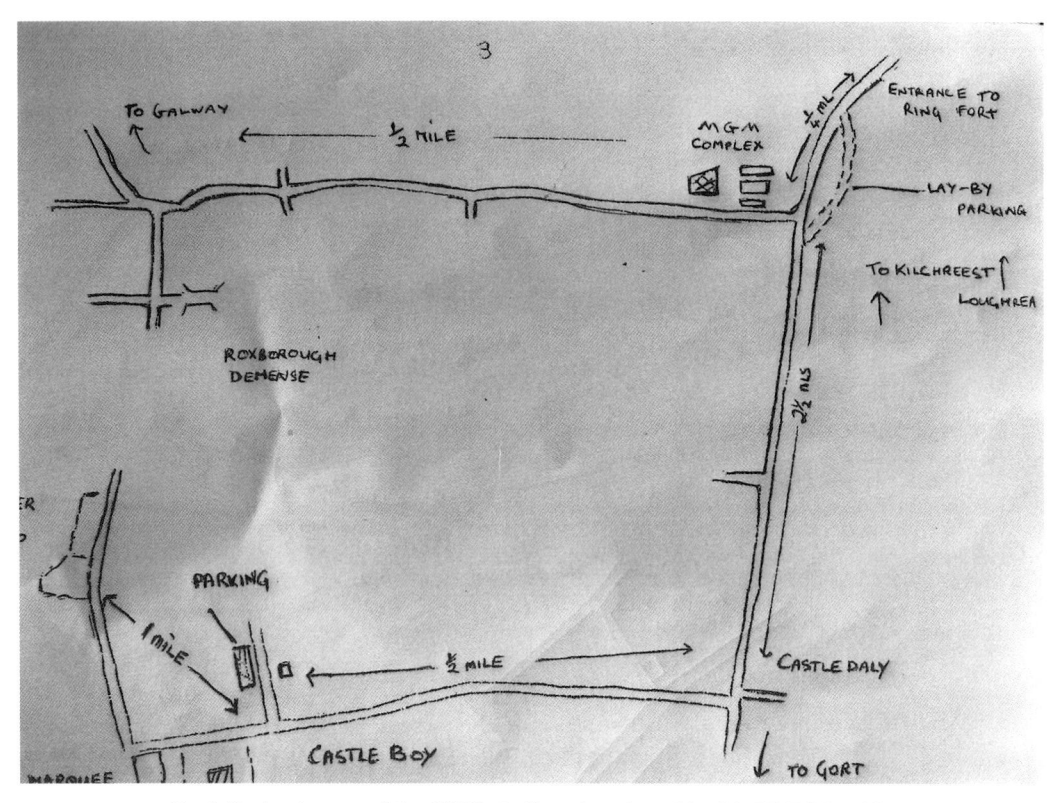

Hugh Harlow's map of the MGM studio, taken from his 'A.L.F.R.E.D.' guide

construction stages, including carpenters like Paddy O'Dea and a Kearns man and Peter Brady and his sons from Moyola Park, at the bottom of College Road in Galway. With them were Paddy Ryan and Martin Ryan and their father, from Shantalla in Galway. After the haybarns were put up by the Keenans of Bagnelstown, loads of canteens and Barna huts were then erected. Members of the fire brigade were out there, full-time, for safety reasons and later on, for cosmetic purposes, when grass had to look glistening and wet, or when fires in the village set had to be extinguished. Ned Waldron remembered Walter Hegarty as being the main fireman, along with Reillys from Loughrea and a family of Dolans from the Docks area of Galway. Some of the best fun they had was when *"we'd see the 'rushes' in the little cinema they had in Kilchreest"*.

Waldron explained that the studio complex didn't consume as much energy as one might think – it was connected to a three-phase line, joined up to its own transformer. They had to go down to 110 volts and there were aluminium buzz bars to take the cameras. *"We stripped it out at the end,"* he said, *"and Krack wanted some of us to go down to Dingle with them afterwards where much of the same crew was involved in the making of 'Ryan's*

Daughter!'" One of those whom Mr. Waldron found easiest to deal with was Clive Donner, the director, describing him as a very reasonable man to work for. Other names that cropped up were those of the three nurses on site (including Mrs. Cahill and Mrs Callanan), and firemen Mike Keary from Loughrea and Michael Reilly from Portumna. The finished product disappointed Waldron. *"There was no story to it. We were sorry, really, because we knew Clive Donner a bit. He stayed in Kilcolgan Castle and his driver was Gerry Connolly. He's dead now, too, but he used to drive John Huston, who stayed in St. Cleran's."*

The big snow scene in *Alfred The Great*, reminiscent of *Dr. Zhivago* (although there's no connection apart from David Lean, its director, being a huge influence on Clive Donner) was filmed at the complex. Waldron remembered the making of those scenes well and said that the 'snowflakes' were actually flitters of white aeroboard. We read elsewhere that the 'snow blanket' on the ground was made entirely from lorryloads of crushed white Connemara marble. That brought about big problems in hot weather because the sun reflected off the marble and actually caused immense discomfort and sunburn to some of the actors and extras.

Pat Barrett from Loughrea was an extra up around Kilchreest and sent us copies of his original receipts from MGM – signed by Hugh Harlow, a significant name that crops up later. The address on both receipts is MGM British Studios, Ltd, c/o Flannery's Buildings, Lough Atalia Road, Galway.

Barrett was an extra for five days as a foot soldier, wore a uniform, costume helmet and high boots and carried a sword and a shield. He had no lines to say, apart from *"roaring and shouting"* and he thinks he saw the initial advertisement concerning the movie in *The Connacht Tribune*. Pay per day was in the order of £8 cash, going up to about £12 a day if you had horsemanship skills, and hairdressers got about a tenner. A canteen served lunch on site and Barrett recalls that firemen were particularly well remunerated. Extras, he said, were definitely in the way of some danger on certain occasions, *"especially from horse soldiers as most of them (UCG students) never rode a horse before. They were doing it because they got more money. Can you just imagine 20 or 30 horses coming at you with a crowd of university students riding them?"*

"On a few occasions we hid behind a ditch when we saw them coming. It was a miracle none of us were killed ... the week I was involved we had a heatwave and between the weight of

VIKING SUMMER

Knockma namestone, 2008.
This namestone, at the entrance to Knockma, was donated by David Burke, editor of *The Tuam Herald* newspaper. It was the location to which Peter Price, Assistant Director on *Alfred The Great*, returned to Galway after a 40-year absence, in June 2008

our clothes and swords, it was hard going. There was a scene where there were two cows pulling a cart and one of them dropped dead with the heat." He recalled a real-life 'battle' in the canteen at one stage, tempers fraying after a 20-minute wait for food. *"A few of the lads from Galway started complaining about the delay and the cat was set amongst the pigeons when one of the canteen staff, who was not Irish, called the Galway lads "ignorant f****ers."* All hell broke loose. *"With that,"* said Pat, *"the real battle started. They jumped over the counter, the canteen staff ran out the door and the lads ran after them. Someone shouted, 'Now get the camera!'"*

That flavour of the impact *Alfred The Great* had on some participants in the Kilchreest/Loughrea hinterland, never mind the assiduous attention to detail paid by Phil Topliss during construction and preparation, mirrors precisely events that unfolded forty miles to the north of the Slieve Aughtys, when the MGM cavalcade set up camp in the magnificently rugged, scenic location at Castlehackett. No stone was left unturned there either and all hands were on deck to ensure that a top-drawer movie would be the outcome.

CHAPTER SIX

Ironically, the 'stones' that were certainly not left unturned on the hill of Knockma, almost equidistant between the villages of Belclare (Corofin parish) and Caherlistrane (itself a parish), were actually as fake as sightings of the Yeti. John Morris of Caltragh is the man who saw the MGM crew making the 'papier-mâché stones and rocks' in a timber-and-wire-mesh frame one day, filling them with a papier mâché mix and leaving them to dry in the glaring sun. That was about all that was faked on this site of the enormous battle of White Horse Hill because every 'i' was dotted and every 't' crossed before Donner shouted, "Action!" By far the biggest undertaking there was the gouging out of the 200-foot-long horse-shape on the hill.

Frank Canavan, who runs the family pub in the village of Belclare, was a student in University College Galway during filming and although he was working in America for most of the action, he told us where the horse was positioned – up on the front of the hill (facing Croagh Patrick, to the north) to the right of the creamery, down near the castle. Amazingly, an aerial shot of the hill taken years later showed the horse's outline, information given to us by Mark Killilea, retired local politician and former TD and MEP, who was astounded when he saw the equine shape quite clearly with his own eyes.

Canavan's public house, Belclare (near Knockma), used as a base when MGM were filming at Castlehackett

VIKING SUMMER

John Morris, member of the Caherlistrane-Kilcoona Group Water Scheme (front, l-r: John Morris, Michael Moran (chairman), Claire McHugh (secretary), Minister Tony Killeen; back, l-r: Noel Higgins, Michael Connolly, Sean Donoghue, Joe Flanagan (an extra in the movie), Vincent Judge, Tom McCabe, Tim Keady, Enda Monaghan and Leo McHugh)

For about five weeks in the summer of '68, John Morris worked on the film set with his tractor and trailer and remembers, with huge amusement, that he got paid £84 for his first week's work. His neighbours, Sarah and Michael Joe Monaghan, were involved as were local men like Joe Muldoon (RIP) from Ballintleva, Pete Burke (Belclare), John Murphy, Paris and Paddy McDermott of Castlehackett

Morris explained that MGM representatives arrived more than a year before any work started, feeling their way and ensuring that the company would be welcome. *"They told my father about it,"* said John, *"but he was sworn to secrecy."* Castlehackett House was burned to the ground in 1923, according to an article written by The Knight of Glin in 1986, when the contents of Castlehacket House were being auctioned off following the death of Percy Paley in 1985. It had been rebuilt in the 1920s.

When the UK branch of MGM, based at Boreham Wood in Hertfordshire, arrived in Castlehackett, only 45 years had passed since the destruction of the 'big house', so an advance party went in ahead, perused the scene and took the political temperature. The presence of a mighty fat wallet, bulging with what Michael Mullery called "clean crispy pound notes" went a long way towards smoothing the road ahead.

Gerard Glynn of Feeragh and Biggera

The view from the top of Knockma, taken beside the grave of General Bernard in 1999. Morgan Glynn, aged 6 months, is in the rucksack enjoying the first of his numerous trips to the top of the hill. Lough Corrib can be seen twinkling in the distance. Bernard, a grandson of Denis Kirwan, was the last in the direct Kirwan line at Castle Hacket and he died in 1956. The following is taken from an obituary of the time and we are grateful to Michael J. Hughes and his book, *History and Folklore of the Barony of Clare* (1997) for this information. "The death occurred on Saturday, August 25th, at his home, Castle Hacket, County Galway, of Lt. Gen. Sir Denis Kirwan Bernard, K.C.B., C.B., C.M.S., D.S.O., a former Governor of Bermuda. He was born in Galway in 1882, son of the late Mr. Percy B. Bernard and Mary, daughter of Denis Kirwan, Castle Hacket. Educated at Eton and Sandhurst, he was gazetted in the Rifle Brigade in 1902, and served throughout the first World War in France, Gallipoli, Salonica and Egypt. He was wounded early in the war and received the C.M.S., the D.S.O. and the Croix de Guerre. He was appointed as a General Staff officer in 1915. He was promoted to the rank of Colonel in 1930 and became a major-general in 1933. In 1939 he became a Lieutenant-general and was knighted."

General Bernard was not long in charge of Bermuda because it was decided early in World War II that the governor should be a civil person rather than a military man. He was pensioned off by the British government and came back to take charge of Castle Hacket until his death, when his nephew, Percy Paley, took over. (photo © Mary J. Murphy)

VIKING SUMMER

'KING ALF HAS HIS VICTORY AFTER ALL', *Connacht Tribune,* Aug 23 1968
A front-page story in *The Connacht Tribune* from August 68, explaining that the industrial unrest that had threatened to upend the smooth sailing of the movie production had been sorted out. The hullabaloo occurred when filming was taking place at Ross Lake and involved student extras, represented by Aidan Heffernan (from the Commerce faculty), as well as MGM personnel. It seems that the students had been agitating for improved pay and conditions, to bring them on par with their fellow extras in the UK. The UCG chaps had also been seeking back pay for the previous 12 weeks during which they had been working out at Roscahill. The phrase 'storm in a teacup' springs to mind…

A large céad míle fáilte was thrown for MGM and *"it was the first time any real money came into the place from the outside"*, according to John Morris, some years before the Teagasc Agricultural Institute was built at the foothills of Knockma. In his article, the Knight of Glin further explained how the Kirwan family of Castlehackett took over the property from the MacHacketts in the 15th century, building up an extremely large trade with French merchants, particularly in the St Malo and La Rochelle areas, eventually establishing a vineyard near Bordeaux where Chateau Kirwan is still a well known name in the Medoc. The mythical king of Knockma, Fin Varra, is famed in the annals, and in modern times Percy Paley became very well known for building up a remarkable library in the 1960s and 70s, having a special interest in genealogical books. When his uncle, Sir Denis Bernard, died unmarried in 1956, after his time spent as Governor and Commander-in-Chief of Bermuda, Paley (son of Denis's sister Frances, who had married George Arthur Paley of Ampton Hall, Suffolk) took over the reins. He was the Lord of the Manor in situ when MGM stumbled into this rich mix of *'Upstairs, Downstairs'.*

Sarah Monaghan explained that Michael Joe didn't remain with the movie as long as he had intended because when filming switched to daytime, he had to revert to his own job, selling

CALLSHEET No.4

Director..............John Smith
Producers...........Barbara Doran
........................Lynne Wilson
........................Kevin Tierney
........................Tristan Orpen Lynch
Production Supervisor.......Jo Homewood

Contacts: Assis. Loc.-J.P.Le Bon:087 3364285
ord.-JulieP&ddn€s- 086
3595901

'LOVE & SAVAGERY'

Production Office, C/o Kilkee Bay Hotel
Kilkee, Co Clare
Tel: 065 9083617   Fax: 065 9060062
Newfoundland Office: 54 Glencoe Drive
Mount Pearl NL, AIN 459
Tel: 001 709 7470306

Date: Thursday 3rd April 2008
Day 4   Out of   30   Dc
Unit Call: 08.00
Breakfast From: 07.00
Sunrise: 07.08   Sunset: 20.20
Weather: Dry with sunny spells. Max. 15 degr

A Bus will stand/by at Logues/Hylands Hotel to transport crew to Unit Base from 07.00.
See transport below for arrangements from other accommodation

SET/DESCRIPTION	SCENE	CAST	DAY	PGs	LOCATION
INT BALLYCLOCHAN/Church Cathleen does her penance	39	2	D4	3/8	Ballyvaughan Church
INT BALLYCLOCHAN/Church Cathleen receives communion	15	2,4,5,6,9,10	D3	3/8	Ballyvaughan Church
INT KINMORE/Moving Bus Cathleen on the Bus. Meets Michael in Kinmore	93	1,2	D14	1 6/8	Ballyvaughan Town Sq.
EXT KINMORE/Phone Booth-Square Michael on the phone w/Kathleen, Bus waiting	92	1	D13		Ballyvaughan Town Sq.
EXT KINMORE VILLAGE Village Life	95		D14		UNIT BASE Burren Coast Hotel Ballyvaughan

CAST	CHARACTER	B/FAST	HAIR	M/U	WARD
Allan Hawco	Michael		11.00	11.15	11.50
Sarah Greene	Cathleen	-	07.00	07.45	07.40
Mark Whelan	Jim Hyland	07.45	-	08.15	08.30
Dylan Smith	Sean Collins	07.45	-	08.35	08.00
Macdara O'Fatharta	Thomas Collins	08.00	08.45	09.00	08.30
Louise Nichol	Mrs Collins	06.50	07.45	07.00	08.15
* Frank Deacy	Father Joseph	07.00	-	07.15	07.45

Call sheets from the movie *'Love and Savagery'* (2008)
This callsheet is taken from the movie, *Love and Savagery,* which was filmed in part on location in Ballyvaughan, County Clare, in May 2008. The picture is a co-production between RTE and Canadian interests and featured a man called Frank Deacy as 'Father Joe'. Deacy is from Galway and has lived in Newfoundland for over thirty-five years. In 1968, he was one of the many UCG student extras who participated in *Alfred The Great.* Interestingly, *Love and Savagery* is also set in 1968 and stars Allan Hawco, Sarah Greene, Mark Whelan, Dylan Smith and Macdara O'Faharta

pools for Gael Linn. His cousin, Pascal Whelan, now deceased, took his place for the duration of the summer.

John Morris told how the film crew did up Matt Keane's (father of Dolores, Sean, Matt and Co.) old house at the foot of the track leading up Knockma, re-roofing it and putting in new windows, to make it habitable for the summer. It was originally a small Protestant Church and Michael Joe has firm memories from 1925 or 1926, when he was a young fellow, of going in around the church with Paddy and the other Murphys and seeing old prayer books

VIKING SUMMER

and missals lying around. The track in from Collins' at the side of the hill off the Caltragh road used to be kept well maintained with cinders, and Protestants from as far away as Annaghdown (and the Palmers and the like) used to make their way to the chapel in along there. The Dean of Tuam came out regularly for services, so it was still in use inside living memory. Sarah Monaghan explained that it used to be called *"Teachín A-máin"*, (Amen House, House of Prayer). Bernie Hession, his old friend and neighbour, told John Morris about that cinder track.

The only land that was used for filming in the Castlehackett locality belonged to Percy Paley, and news of the movie spread like a bush fire. There was a big meeting in Canavan's pub where people went forward for interviews with MGM, having known for some weeks that they'd have to have long hair to have any chance of being taken on the books. Gerard Glynn, a small boy in Feeragh at the time, clearly remembers his uncle, Joe Moran and his neighbour, Joseph Cunningham, having straggly beards and the chat in the village consisting of nothing but *"Alfie, Alfie, Alfie."*

John Morris spoke of Mattie McTigue's shop (father of quarry operator, Gary McTigue), which he moved over to the hill while the filming was on. *"It was hard on the soldiers out from Renmore,"* explained John, *"because their commander wouldn't let them stop on their way out to the lorries bringing them back into the barracks in Galway. Anyway, they got around that one too because Mattie wrote the price of everything – apples, oranges, chocolates, ice creams - up on a sign and the soldiers just threw the exact amount of money to him as they were passing, without stopping."*

There was great money in it, for sure, but the work could be hot and tiring during the day and bitterly cold at night. John Morris said that he saw Joe Raftery from Corofin dressed up in his raggy Saxon costume one night, around 4 or 5 a.m. sitting up in the branch of a tree on the left as you go up the hill where the reservoir is, and doesn't know how he didn't die with the cold. *"There was no protection at all in the Saxon clothes. They were just a bunch of rags."* That's the level of insistence the film producers maintained, using only the most authentic of costumes. Morris saw an even more obsessive aspect to that insistent drive for realism when crew members were made to cover up ash trees, because that particular species of tree was anachronistic to Alfred's time in the Wessex of the 870s A.D. Utter madness, but Morris saw them erect scaffolding during the 'great leaf cover-up' and it can't be said that Bernard Smith's pet project floundered for the want of accuracy.

Clive Donner on the Shannon, filming the opening sequences with the longships, accompanied by Alex Thomson and Tony Spratling (photo courtesy of Frances Russell, British Society of Cinematographers)

VIKING SUMMER

John Morris, Caltragh, Caherlistrane
John Morris of Caltragh in full flight, doing a fine impersonation of a movie director himself…
He worked on the set of *Alfred The Great* all through the summer of 1968 and made an extraordinary
£84 during his first week with MGM, using his tractor and trailer rig.
(photo © Tadhg Keady)

Morris and the Monaghans recalled other participants like Paddy Flanagan, Paddy Murphy, Joe Raftery, Willie Cunningham, Sean O'Brien, Mick Fahy, Tim Lawless (RIP), Joe Flanagan and Seamus McHugh from Cortoon. Although not an extra, Charlie Coen from Corrandrum had his own brief encounter with MGM one night when he got a puncture in his van at Claretuam crossroads at 3am. He was travelling from Sligo and had no spare wheel so was delighted when a Ford Thunderbird 100 horsepower screeched to a halt and came to his assistance. It was a very, very fast motorcar indeed.

This good Samaritan was working on *Alfred The Great* (we don't have the name) and reached speeds of 130mph going through Loughgeorge, said Charlie. There was a fair in Galway that same morning and the road was packed with livestock, causing the driver to brake hard and

Props from *'Love and Savagery'*, Ballyvaughan 2008
One of the many old cars, buses and agricultural machines used as 'props' in the joint RTE/Canadian co-production, *Love and Savagery,* partially filmed on location in Ballyvaughan in the heart of the Burren, County Clare in May 2008, featuring Frank Deacy as Father Joe

swerve to avoid the animals. Mr. Coen remembers the driver turning to him saying, *'Isn't there a lot of wildlife on the road this morning?'* "He wanted to bring me out to Claretuam with the spare wheel but I wasn't about to risk my life again!"

The powerful filming lights, *"brutes"*, they called them, have lived long in the memories of Castlehackett locals, often keeping Sarah Monaghan and her friends awake at night. Incidentally, her daughter, Margie (Margaret) Naughton, actually had a little dog at the time called 'Prunie', after Prunella Ransome, so taken were they by the frisson of excitement surrounding the movie.

Some of the neighbouring men who helped dig out the 200-foot white horse were Martin Kennedy, Paddy Murphy, Paddy Flanagan, Frank Creaven and Sean Quinn, Patrick Hynes and Michael Hynes, all of whom gave their sweat to authenticate the real horse in Berkshire, the edges of which are cleaned out regularly in a process called "scouring", a phrase that actually turns up in the book, *Tom Brown's Schooldays.*

VIKING SUMMER

George Best, member of the victorious Manchester United 1968 team and former 'beau' of Miss Sinead Cusack, according to his own autobiography (Photographer unknown)

The women of the locality were restricted by domestic and farm duties from spending too much time on the hill, but Sarah Monaghan did get to observe events on the very first night of filming, along with Josie Whelan, Michael Collins, Dermot Morris, Sally Corless, Timmy and Mary. Nurse O'Grady and the Canavan women (mother Kitty, Kay Newell, Julie and Ann,

RIP) along with father, Batty and Frank, were involved tangentially, too in their pub business.

The logistical organisational skills of *Alfred The Great*'s back- up support staff and crew, all appear to have been tip-top, up to and including the provision and supply of food and drink for the enormous throngs of people who gathered on a hill in the middle of nowhere. John Morris spoke of how he often saw up to 1,500 people fed and then cleared away well inside an hour. Leo Courtney, from Pollnahallia, remembers the film vividly and recalls the time his pal, Joe Flanagan came over to cut the hay that summer, with a big long new beard, with his friends, Michael Judge and Joe and Jackie Lardner. Courtney is a strong GAA *aficionado* but he loves other codes too and has in his possession a copy of the 1968 match programme when Manchester United (with the mighty George Best) won the European soccer championship the same year that *Alfred* was filmed. Interestingly enough, Best talks in his biography of the dates he had with Sinead Cusack, who played Edith in that, her debut film.

Michael John Hughes of Belclare was in Caherlistrane that summer and is a well known writer of history books about Knockma and its hinterland. He recalled two men from his village, Mick Mulroe and Michael McHugh, who were extras, and shared a famous yarn from the time. A local wit, Patsy Burke RIP, was invited by some film crew to take a spin in a helicopter and when he appeared reluctant to do so, someone said, *'If your time is up, your time is up.'* Patsy's reply was, *'What if the pilot's time is up?'* "*That joke has spread nationally since but the original seems to have been on that occasion,*" explained Hughes.

You could hold a party in a telephone box for the amount of women we've managed to talk to who were directly involved in the film as extras and that's why it was with great delight that we received a communication from internationally renowned poet, Leland Bardwell. She was an extra in crowd scenes in *Alfred The Great* for some three weeks and recalled the event with some amusement. *"David Hemmings had to cross a stream on stepping stones and every time he did it he slipped into the water. His line was 'I need some more villagers' but after his umpteenth time falling, he shouted out, 'I need some more f***ing villagers'! My daughter also got a couple of days (in the film) as did my three small sons. It was like an endless holiday. We camped in a field near a ruin in Moycullen and the weather was brilliant."*

Ms Bardwell's involvement with Alfred didn't end there, however, because years later, an extraordinary coincidence occurred. *"I was invited to Bogota, in Colombia, to give a reading*

VIKING SUMMER

Clive Donner and the purpose-built longships on the Shannon
(photo courtesy of Frances Russell, British Society of Cinematographers)

and the day I arrived in the hotel I put on the telly and there we were, cavorting down the beautiful Galway hills, as happy as bedamned – and that was 1998."

Tony Melia of Harrow in Middlesex was an extra, out at Ross Lake, between Moycullen and Oughterard at Roscahill, and remembered that they were plagued by midges, while Michael Cooley from Galway, six weeks old at the time, was one of the babies who played Alfred's son in the movie, being paid £26 for his troubles. Michael 'Chick' Gillen, barber and coach of Ireland's Olympic boxer, Francis Barrett, enjoyed his time as a fireman on location and his most vivid recall concerns the magnificent quality of the food and the permanent smell of smoke in the blazing hot sun, day in, day out. We've seen the time and expertise that was expended on all aspects of the film but that paled in comparison with the effort that was put into the making of the Viking longships. MGM could not have bettered their preparations in this regard.

They were multi-purpose vessels, used for exploration, the planks on the floor of the ship being kept loose so as to double up for storage purposes. When land was reached, the planks were lifted and used as gangplanks. Finally, those same planks were used - when stacked up against each other - to form the rough structures that held skins and pelts, making temporary shelter and accommodation for the Danes. Some 120 men from the Irish Army's Southern and Western Command, based in Athlone, underwent training as oarsmen in these 80 foot longboats. They were built by Frederiksens, the famous Danish ship-building firm, and according to Hugh Harlow, Production Manager on *Alfred The Great*, Mike Turk was involved at an important level as well. He was a well known boatman for the film industry from Kingston-on-Thames, and the two mighty sea craft were eventually sailed up around the southern tip of Ireland and brought up along the Shannon to their Athlone destination.

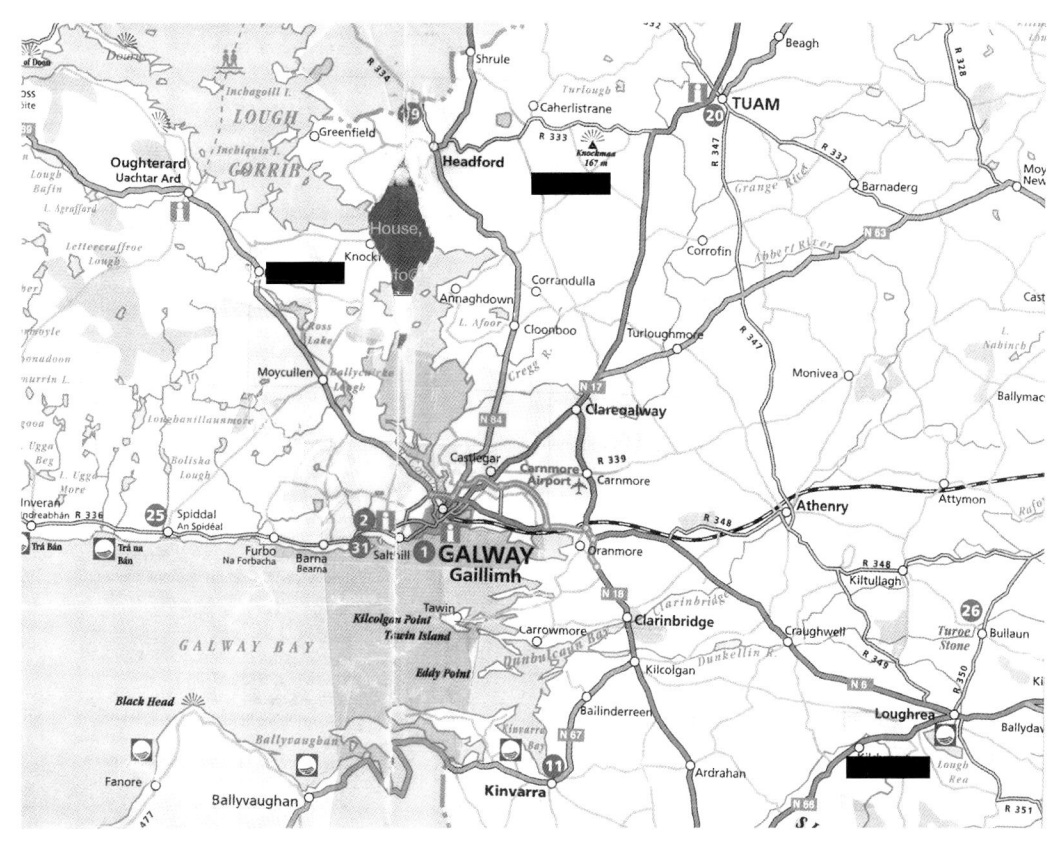

Map of the west of Ireland, showing film locations at Knockma, Roscahill and Kilchreest

CHAPTER SEVEN

Hugh Harlow's role as Unit Production Manager – his first job at that level in the industry – was substantial, running from early January 1968 through to administering the production to completion in November. While in Galway he stayed with Bernard and Marcia Cassidy from Barna, friends to this day. He spoke of the passing of a number of key players, including Alex Thomson, whose cinematography gave such an *"artistic and moody look to the film...* and *"though it wasn't received very enthusiastically in box-office terms it was still a very fine technically made movie with superb acting talents."* One of Harlow's first tasks was to put together a booklet, 'A.L.F.R.E.D' (Administration-Locations-Facilities-Routes-Explanation-Details) which contained all of the information that was needed by MGM's production people upon their arrival in Galway. It's a superb example of how to organise the making of a movie.

VIKING SUMMER

Chief Superintendent Colleran was the most senior point of contact for MGM in the Force; Doctor O'Beirne from the Crescent was the medical person in Galway; Dr. J.J. Keane was the equivalent in Athlone for filming on the Shannon, and the dentist attached to the film was A. D. Browne with an address on Eyre Sqauare. MGM's point of connection with CIE was with its managing Director, Mr. F. Lemass, and in Galway, CIE's area sales manager was J.N. Smithwick. In the transport section (page 6), Abbey Delivery Services were listed under Pantechnicons; Faherty's in Moycullen provided coaches; Carroll's garage in Galway looked after the minibuses; Dan Ryan's cars were hired, as were vehicles from Higgin's Ford garage in town. McMullen Bros and Shannon Oil (Shell and B.P) helped look after the logistics of fuel distribution.

We won't list every single name and snippet from Harlow's expansive guide but certain names do hop off the page, such as Sean O'Modhrain, the link man between the film and the Department of Defence (in Parkgate Street, Dublin) in his capacity as Secretary to that Department. A Colonel Griffin was in charge in the Barracks in Renmore, being Officer Commanding of the 1st Battalion, and Commandant Erraught was the MGM contact. His counterpart in Athlone was Commandant Gleeson and the MGM liaison officer was a Colonel P.J. Kearns (retired).

The film's personnel list of 250 employees (on allowance) showed all of the guest houses and locations in which crew from the film stayed and Hugh's booklet adds to that, giving the names of the main hotels where some of the more senior MGM members resided during filming. The Great Southern in Eyre Square was then under the managership of Mr. R.J.C. Murphy, the Odeon just along from the Square was managed by W. Edwards and some of the other venues included were the Eglinton Hotel (home of Twiggs nightclub in later years), the Golf Links Hotel in Salthill, the Gresham in Dublin's O'Connell Street, Haydens in Ballinasloe plus The Prince of Wales, the Hodson Bay and the Shamrock Lodge, all three in Athlone, used during the filming at Killinure on the Shannon.

After all of the build-up and hoopla, filming finally began on May 23rd, 1968, as per scheduled in Harlow's magnificently concise and extraordinarily detailed movie handbook.

To Fish Ponds we go, the local name for the area near Paddy Stewart in Eskershanore outside Kilchreest, where the first tranche of filming lasted fom May 23rd to June 30th, the second from July 18th to 29th, and the final segment running from September 1st to 13th, making a grand total of 38 days intermittent filming up around Stewart's farm.

There was a 24-hour, seven-day security service on site with two men carrying out two twelve-hour shifts, upped to three men plus a guard dog on the night shift and on Sundays – when no filming took place.

That same security function was carried out by Frank Higgins and his comrades at Castlehackett, a man who retains friendly memories of Jim Norton, Thanet in the movie. Gort guards listed were Superintendent Nolan and Sergeant Mulreaney, and Sergeant Kilcommins was on hand from Peterswell. The medical and first aid plans left nothing to chance either because Dr. P. Joyce, Mrs. P. Joyce and Dr. Millette from Ardrahan worked in cooperation with the film, Mrs Joyce to remain in the MGM Complex when Dr. Joyce went to the main unit or to other locations. All eventualities were provided for, the nurses being Mrs. Phil Callanan from Cahergal, Craughwell and Mary Brennan from Kilchreest, their presence requested continuously on site, each working alternate days.

The filming location on Larkin's land at Deerpark in Kilchreest was where exterior scenes 74, 78, 79, 82, 83, 84 were done and pre-construction began there on May 1st. It lasted for 38 days through to June 7th after which shooting of exterior shots of Wilton Manor took place from June 10th to 13th. That's just a taster of the exquisite detail of the scene-by-scene beakdown that's contained in Harlow's masterpiece and the exact same detail was applied to Castlehackett, which Harlow was also responsible for organising.

On location at Knockma was the exterior of Ashdown Battle (the charge of White Horse Hill); the King's tent; the exterior pond which Christy Dooley explained had to be heated for Hemmings from a nearby kettle, the country lane that was used for Ambush B; and scenes number 18 all the way through to 45, plus scene 121.

Camp preparation time there is also described in Hugh's guide – construction at Castlehackett, including the road and camp erection – took place in the four weeks between May 13th, 1968 and June 10th, with more pre-construction during the three weeks from June 10th to June 30th. Filming at the side of Knockma was done in three tranches – from July 1st to 13th; July 15th and 16th, and for one day on July 17th. The lease period between MGM and Percy Paley was from May 20th to August 10th, 1968.

VIKING SUMMER

The administration of that segment of the film was done entirely on location at Castlehackett, hence the unmerciful amount of tents and equipment that were put in place to support the weight of the project. The main service road on the hill had a huge parking bay with a subsidiary service road for the filming area, plus a parking bay for generators and essential equipment vehicles. The maximum number of marquees and caravans was required, and the electricity was provided by the ESB to serve the camp site only, the output being 45 kilowatts. Two telephones were to be installed in the production office caravan (numbers to be advised) and the water supply was serviced by a pipeline from Mr. Paley's spring. A tank was to be built to gather and store piped water.

Local gardai who were named as contacts in the booklet included Superintendent Clifford and Sergeant Gillespie in Tuam, as well as Sergeant Timlin in Headford. A night watchman was to be on site and the medical back-up included Dr. P. Joyce from Ardrahan (resident on site), Nurse T. O'Grady, SRN, of Castlehackett (resident on site), plus Nurse Cora McNamara from Shop Street in Tuam and an ambulance and driver (Pat O'Neill), c/o Dr. McHugh in Taylor's Hill in Galway.

The set dressing in Castlehackett – the film company notes called it Castle Hacket – was as per Art Department, drawn up by Michael Stringer and dressed by the inimitable, unforgettable and, later on, Oscar nominee, Patrick McLoughlin. In 1970 Mr. McLoughlin was nominated for an Academy award for his work on Art Direction and Set Decoration in the movie, *Anne Of The Thousand Days* (1969). Prior to that, back in 1965, Patrick had been co-nominated in the same categories for the 1964 movie, *Becket*, about the life and times of Thomas à Becket. The last sighting we have of Patrick McLoughlin, from a professional point of view, concerns his work on *Treasure Island* in 1982. He had purchased a property in County Clare, with the guidance of Henry Comerford, after *Alfred the Great*.

The road contractor on Knockma was Paddy O'Grady (under MGM's Fred Bennett) and the army liaison was Cmdt P. Egan, who also oversaw Frank Higgins, Sonny Creavan and Pa Costello.

One of the many structures built by MGM when filming at Castlehackett was a huge ramp up the hill from the dairy, across to Ballydotia on Sean McHugh's land. *"That was used,"* explained John Morris, *"as a rostrum for the cameras when they were up high, filming a battle scene down below. It was lit up at night and I remember there was a big drop underneath to the ground, under where the railing and tracks were for the camera runs."* Morris and Higgins recalled seeing Ned Cash (who kept his horses at Kilchreest on Lal Murphy's land) training the horses to "fall dead" for the battle scenes, on an area where local man, Paddy O'Grady, had brought a lorry load of white fine sand that was used for the animals to collapse upon. The same man made the road up the hill and brought the rubbish, loaded each evening, off to the dump.

Hugh Harlow, who entered the film industry at 16 and came up through the ranks of the Hammer movies, met up with Ian McKellen again as recently as 1995 when both men worked on *Rasputin*, filmed in Budapest and St. Petersburg. Harlow has exceedingly positive memories of Henry Comerford from those halcyon days forty years ago and described him as *"a great source of wisdom and down to earth humour."* Harlow worked on two James Bond films – *Octopussy* and *The World Is Not Enough* – and spent ten years working in Canada. That connection forms a link with Frank Deacy, former UCG student extra, who returned from his home in Canada in May/June 2008, having been flown back by a film company in which he played the role of Fr. Joe in the movie, *Love and Savagery*. Deacy's adviser for the priestly role was Fr. Des Ford, priest in Ballyvaughan, whose own family actually had another dog named after *Alfred The Great* in 1968.

It's palpably obvious that Hugh Harlow went to every length possible to set up a perfect shooting schedule for *Alfred The Great*, and praised the cooperation he received from Fr. O'Connor in Kilchreest and Enda Rohan of the Department of Posts and Telegraphs (and his wife, Kathleen) for the fantastic telephone system, but there was one thing that was outside even his amazing organisation capabilities – the weather. Harlow explained, having been brought onto the film by Roy Parkinson, Executive Producer (who died last November at 92), that *"we were there in the west of Ireland expecting damp conditions, which is one of the main reasons Ireland was chosen, only to be greeted by one of the hottest summers on record."* Of Lord Killanin, Harlow has warm memories, recalling that he was a wonderful guiding hand at all times, being especially wise and helpful when the time came to negotiate the use of land owned by numerous farmers in the Ross Lake region where the striking phalanx battle scenes were filmed. Another whom Harlow praises highly is Moira Colleran, then assistant manager of the Great Southern Hotel and one *"who was a tremendous asset all during filming."*

Harlow helped us understand the distinction between MGM UK and the parent company in

VIKING SUMMER

the US by explaining the set-up thus: MGM was an American company producing and distributing its films. They had a base in London at Boreham Wood, and revenues from MGM-produced and distributed movies went back to HQ in Hollywood. The UK section of MGM would hire out studio stages, offices, dressing rooms, facilities, studio technicians and construction personnel and reap the revenue into sterling. By all accounts (including his own in the *Photoplay* magazine interview of March 1969), it was Bernard Smith who had the germ of an idea to make *Alfred*, a notion which he took to MGM/Hollywood. They liked it, Smith was hired as an independent producer to make the film on their behalf and he came to MGM/UK to set the ball rolling. The production would have been officially financed by MGM-Hollywood but based out of MGM-Boreham Wood, and funded through a sterling account as far as wages and facilities were concerned.

"We were employed by and on a MGM/UK letterhead," Hugh said, *"and our immediate boss was Bernard Smith. Sadly, as you know, the further wheels of fate were turning. The television industry was taking its hold on 'big screen' turnout and revenues were dropping. There was a takeover in the boardrooms of MGM-Hollywood, and, as well as selling off prime 'back studio' lot space and sets, costumes, props and the like in Los Angeles, one further major decision was made. That was to close down their 115-acre site, the largest film studio facility in London, and that led to demolition and closure of MGM/UK. And, now, the $64,000 question - did the failure of* Alfred The Great *bring MGM-UK to its knees? No, I don't think it had any bearing on this closure,"* said Hugh Harlow. *"It was just a matter of being in the wrong place at the wrong time."*

CHAPTER EIGHT

Peter Price, wife Teresa in the centre and her sister, Renie, at Knockma in 2008

Peter Price was one of the senior MGM people who worked on the film, being 1st Assistant Director to Clive Donner, and he made a return visit to Galway in June 2008 after a forty-year absence, to retrace his steps to Castlehackett. It was his job to control the smooth-running of the film on the set, known in the business as 'the floor', and to make sure that they kept up to schedule. He was accompanied by his wife, Teresa – who was with him in Ireland for six months in 1968 - and her sister, Renie.

VIKING SUMMER

Declan Jennings, responsible for many of the townland name stones that are popping up around Knockma, Lough Hacket, Castlehacket, etc

We drove out from Galway city, taking the N17 towards Tuam, and as Knockma loomed ever larger Peter Price grew more animated. As we rounded the sharp, dangerous bend just before the right turn into the woods at Knockma, he exclaimed, *"Here we are now. This is it. The white horse was further on, always to our right as we approached. There was a pub too, wasn't there?"* (Canavan's in Belclare). *"I was never in it but the camera crew used to go there at lunchtime and get 'three parts' and give me and Clive a bit of a rough time when they came back,"* he smiled. In the woods at Knockma the editor of *The Tuam Herald* newspaper, David Burke, met the Price entourage and took some photographs at the name stone at the entrance, donated by Mr. Burke. Declan Jennings from Bohercuill is responsible for many of those carved townland identity stones.

Clive Donner asked Peter Price to work with him on *Alfred The Great*, as they'd collaborated on many films over the years, including the Edgar Wallace series they'd made in Merton Park Studios in the early 1960s. He'd just made *Nothing But the Best* with Clive Donner and *The Mulberry Bush*, and Price had been on *Shalako* in Spain with Brigitte Bardot and Sean Connery immediately prior to *Alfred*.

Peter Price has an industry track record that stretches back almost sixty years to 1949, when we first came across a mention of his name in connection with a film called *The Glass*

Mountain. He spoke extremely highly of Clive Donner. *"He put everything into the film,"* he said, and singled him out for particular praise for the lengthy tracking shot towards the beginning of the movie. It's the one where the horseman gallops towards the chapel as Alfred is about to be ordained. That shot would still be unusual today, explained Price, and was only possible because the entire side of the MGM studio complex at Kilchreest was left open. Michael Stringer designed that aspect of the studio and that scene was praised years later by his colleague, Norman Dorme, it being based on the origins of filming done in the old days in Los Angeles where natural light was a highly praised asset.

Although Price can't put his finger on any one specific reason why *Alfred The Great* wasn't a successful movie, he's aware of small incidents here and there that may have contributed to its failure. Little things by themselves but, when added together, they may have tipped the balance. For instance, we'd learned that Clive Donner had wanted all of his actors, including the stars, to remain unwashed and unshaven during filming, to better give a realistic grotty, sticky, stenchy, medieval 'look' to the picture, but he was overruled on that. There was also a plan to get David Hemmings to use a permanent tonsure instead of having an unsuitable wig fitted every day, but that fell through, too. Price saw wobbles in the production from pretty early on, but the project steamed ahead, notwithstanding his and others' unease over certain matters. Nothing worked one-hundred-per-cent according to plan, including the non-cooperation of the weather, which had been expected to have been grey, drizzly and gloomy. That's what Donner and Smith wanted but instead they got relentless blue skies.

Clive Donner had also intended to shoot the entire movie with a long-focus lens but that didn't happen and many observers have suggested that the cast was completely unsuitable. Possibly so, but Peter Price explained how that might easily have happened. It wasn't unusual in those days, the 1960s, to cast one actor, the main super-duper star, to carry the entire weight of the movie. They would be expected to draw in the crowds to fill the cinema seats, practically by themselves. In that light, it made a certain amount of sense to cast Hemmings as Alfred, not because he was the actor best suited to the part – quite clearly he wasn't – but he had gigantic pulling 'star power' following his immense success in Antonioni's *Blow-Up.* Cometh the hour, cometh the man. Price further elaborated by suggesting that although all of the names in the cast were fine exponents of the art of acting, they were perhaps not best picked for that actual film.

VIKING SUMMER

"The movie business is just that," he explained, *"a business. That's how it's run and that's how decisions are made. You have to keep that in mind at all times."* And yes indeed, he did confirm that the ratio of one success to nine flops is the rule of thumb in the industry, so *Alfred* was merely a normal cinematic casualty. When pressed, Price said that a more mature actor might have been more suited to the role. *"I knew David Hemmings quite well. He was a very, very clever man who died only recently."*

He is well aware of the effect that its failure had on Clive Donner - we read earlier that the director didn't work in the industry for years after its release. In fact, Price and Donner might have worked together again on the film that actually marked Donner's return back to the business (it was about Vampires), but Peter was working on *Valentino* by then. It was the mid-70s and Rudolf Nureyev was in that movie, on which Price had been promoted to Production Manager. Mr. Price is a loyal colleague and was careful to explain how successful and in demand Clive Donner had been at his peak when he was a much sought-after director responsible for films like *Here We Go Round The Mulberry Bush*.

Price talked too about how unsuitable it was to have attempted a big film like *Alfred The Great* with just one stunt coordinator, Paul Stader. *"I told that to all the Heads of Department at the first production meeting we had,"* a meeting that was held - we think - in the Great Southern. *"In contrast, I had just come off a film in Spain with Sean Connery* (Shalako), *and they had both British and Spanish stuntmen and horses that were trained to fall left and right, by just pulling a rein."* He laughed as he recalled the time when one of Alfred's stuntmen, Vic Armstrong, a young man then, decided to train a falling horse with Jimmy Lodge. (This may well have been the same horse that John Morris of Caltra saw manoeuvring for ages on the fine sand that had been delivered in a lorry load by O'Grady). *"They trained him for weeks,"* laughed Price, *"but the bloody horse just wouldn't fall down. They nick-named him 'Failure'. And this was the one and only falling horse we had in the whole picture!"* As it happens, Armstrong went on to become one of the most famous stuntmen in the world, going on to appear in James Bond – and other – films.

According to Mr. Price, Clive Donner gave Alex Thomson, the cinematographer and cameraman, his first picture as DOP (Director of Photography) on *Mulberry Bush* and then he continued those services on *Alfred*. In Galway, Price lived in a new house which was opposite the hospital *"and of course all the crew invited their families to stay with them, including myself"*, an arrangement that was deemed more cost-effective than long-term

THE VILLAGE INN, KILCHREEST
Known as Jack Glynn's pub in 1968, this venue was the social hub around which everything revolved when filming was taking place in the locality during the summer. The MGM studio at Eskershanore is a little more than a mile away, in the Gort direction, and David Hemmings and his colleagues spent many happy hours in this pub in between scenes. If only the walls could talk…
(photo © Mary J. Murphy)

hotel accommodation. Free fuel was also the order of the day for film personnel, but that was also done with the intention that it would be cheaper than providing a fleet of vehicles and/or drivers.

The petrol was supplied by the studio from a pump in a garage in the centre of Galway and it was widely recognised that that facility was misused on occasion, a facility which extended to spouses and visitors who often drove over from England for 'top ups'. There was also a facility at the petrol station to view 'rushes', (scenes that had been filmed the previous day) and in the evening, when the film crew would gather to view the rushes, many often availed of the free telephones in the office above. It's not the end of the world, a free phone call here and there, but when many people do it too often, over a period of six months, to all parts of the globe, it eventually adds up. Perhaps then, the finances of *Alfred The Great* became an issue for all the wrong reasons and maybe the movie died from a death by a

"Alfred the Great" Historical Brochures

Comprehensive "ALFRED THE GREAT" historical brochures have been especially prepared in Great Britain, and have been distributed to over 1000 amusement editors of major Canadian and American newspapers, and to 750 college editors and campus radio station general managers.

Historical Relevance

Host a special screening of "ALFRED THE GREAT" for local high school and college history classes. Because of "ALFRED's" overall historical accuracy, such a screening would serve as an invaluable visual aid to teachers in making medieval history palatable to students.

Medieval Costume Extravaganza

Promote an "ALFRED THE GREAT" *costume party* in your lobby, and award prizes for the most ingenious and accurate medieval garb.

Special Open-end Interviews

David Hemmings, Prunella Ransome, Michael York and Clive Donner have recorded open-end interviews especially tailored for today's young radio audiences. Your local disc jockey will be receptive to programming these interviews, made on location, during his peak listening periods.

Please order your interview record, available free, from

------- CUT OUT AND MAIL -------

Dick Strout, Inc.
P.O. Box 907, Beverly Hills, California.

Please send .... copies of the FREE David Hemmings, Prunella Ransome, Michael York and Clive Donner "Alfred The Great" Interview Records to:

MANAGER..........
THEATRE..........
ADDRESS..........
CITY, STATE, ZIP..........

MGM's PROMOTION/PRESS MATERIAL
From MGM's press book we see the delightful lengths that were gone to in order to promote *Alfred The Great* following its release in July 1969. There were essay contests, the promotion of the 'Alfred Look' in hairstyling, ATG Historical brochures were printed for primary and secondary schools (with the emphasis placed heavily on the US and Canadian markets – Ireland rarely got a mention, with filming in Galway often being slotted in under a "UK location"), and medieval costume extravaganzas were encouraged. It was carefully pointed out at all times that the film was rated M (for mature audiences) and indeed it was refused a certificate by the Irish censor, briefly, on its release in '69, until some minor amendments were made. The film cleverly aligned itself on some occasions with education, maintaining that *Alfred The Great* would be an ideal film to show in high school and college history classes. Get this for a hard sell, taken directly from their own promotional material: "Because of *Alfred's* overall historical accuracy, such a screening would serve as an invaluable visual aid to teachers in making medieval history palatable to students." It didn't work, unfortunately, but it was a very fine idea.

Everything and anything could be bought with *Alfred* logos, including De-Luxe Sectional Valances at $21.50 each; 3-piece Streamers at the same price and cinema usher badges at a mere 50 cent per item. Added to that were insert cards, window cards, plus one-, three- and six-sheet displays, topped off by the glory of Hi-Rise Standees at $9.95, Extension Poles at $1.50 and Day-Glo Title Displays, no price given.

AUDIO-VISUAL AIDS

THEATRE TRAILER—

The theatre trailer available from your National Screen Service branch will keep potential patrons looking for the arrival of "Alfred The Great" at your local theatre.

RADIO SPOTS—

The radio spots, one 60-second, one 30-second, will sell today's audience, especially those under 25. These are available gratis from your MGM field press representative.

TELEVISION SPOTS—

The 60- and 20-second television spots available free from your MGM field press representative will start viewers talking long before "Alfred The Great" comes to town.

LIVE RADIO SPOTS

60 SECOND LIVE ANNOUNCEMENT SPOT

Announcer: Ninth century England was a vast battleground. It was a country at war with itself. Saxon against Norman — Peasant against Noble — Bandit against all. But the greatest threat came from the brutal Vikings of the north. Relentlessly, they beat the divided country into submission — Until all the English had left was a starving army of peasants, led by a twenty-two-year-old boy. He was Alfred, King of Wessex — ALFRED THE GREAT! Metro-Goldwyn-Mayer presents, David Hemmings, Michael York, and Prunella Ransome in — ALFRED THE GREAT! He was a scholar, in a time of ignorance — A warrior, who hated war — A King, and a common man. He led a starving nation to victory over the fiercest fighting men on earth! In over one thousand years of English history only one King has ever been called Great — ALFRED THE GREAT! In color, this picture has been rated M — Suggested for Mature Audiences.

30 SECOND LIVE ANNOUNCEMENT SPOT

Announcer: Metro-Goldwyn-Mayer presents — David Hemmings, Michael York, and Prunella Ransome in — ALFRED THE GREAT! He was a Scholar, in a time of ignorance — A warrior, who hated war — A King, and a common man. He led a starving nation to victory over the fiercest fighting men on earth — The vikings! In over one thousand years of English history, only one King has ever been called Great .... ALFRED THE GREAT! In color, this picture has been rated M — Suggested for mature audiences.

The "Alfred Look" In Hair Styling

Through well-known men's hair styling salons, promote the ever-popular "ALFRED LOOK." Long hair is currently very much in vogue with the 12-to-26 set, and this tie-in is sure to wow the youth market in your hamlet!

Fashion Accessories

Medallions and pendants are being worn extensively by the under-25'ers today. Tie-in with leading jewelry, novelty and psychedelic shops and promote "ALFRED THE GREAT" fashion accessories. Make your town swing with medieval fashion!

The "Now" Look in Fashion

The "now" look in fashion is remarkably similar to the 9th Century costumes sported by King Alfred and his subjects. Through local mod boutiques, sponsor a teen-oriented "ALFRED THE GREAT" FASHION EXPO and capture the imagination of your town's "with it" crowd!

VIKING SUMMER

thousand cuts, rather than from one fell swoop? We just don't know. Nobody does.

CHAPTER NINE

CONCLUSION

The US première of the film took place in Cleveland (Ohio) on July 2nd 1969 with a full release on October 8th that same year. In Dublin it ran in the Adelphi. A Galway contingent (Henry Comerford, Ronnie O'Gorman, Bobby Molloy, Christy Dooley) went to the Odeon in Leicester Square on its UK release. It was roundly trounced and the critics gave it both barrels, annoyed and perplexed that a film with such an amazing wealth and depth of acting, directorial and cinematic expertise available to it could have produced such a ridiculous "turkey".

A review from *The New York Times*, written by Vincent Canby, captures perfectly the tone in most of the reviews that greeted the release of *Alfred The Great*. Helmets on, here we go.

Although he allowed that the film does have a few good things in it, *"as soon as someone opens his mouth, you're aware that you're lost in an exotic movie genre that has proved to be the undoing of almost every creditable director in the last 40 years, with the possible exceptions of Cecil B. de Mille and Sergei Eisenstein."* It gets worse, a lot worse. *"Unlike de Mille,"* he continues, *"Donner has no genius for transforming epic narratives into exalted comic strips, and unlike Eisenstein, he is no master of montage. Donner, the director of two decently contemporary comedies (Nothing But The Best and What's New Pussycat?) and his screenwriters, Ken Taylor and James R. Webb, have visualised the story of Alfred as a sort of Old-English western in which, stranger still, a devoutly Christian Freud confronts the Druid mentality."* It continues - *"Apparently finding the Anglo-Saxon chronicles too skimpy for their needs, Donner and his associates have used an unnamed novel by Eleanor Shipley Duckett as their principal text."* His conclusion is of the poleaxing type, piercing to the very essence of the deep flaw embedded within the movie: *"The film is effective neither on bearskin nor battlefield, neither as conjecture nor as history. Donner hasn't staged his battles as much as he has choreographed them – with all of the unlikely precision of Rockettes routines."*

"The dialogue is of the sort," continued Canby, *"expected from movie characters who wassail too much from hollowed steer horns, and stuffed with subsidiary information not easily dramatized. Thus are covered Alfred's intellectual achievements: 'We need a book in our own Saxon tongue.'"*

VIKING SUMMER

We might as well take it to the bitter end: *"David Hemmings, who plays Alfred, has rather poppy eyes and even reads some lines as Bette Davis might. Prunella Ransome, a lovely, freckled girl, is his unhappy hot-blooded queen, and Michael York is Guthrum, the Danish king. According to the color print I saw, they are all quite green."* That's the end of Vincent Canby and *The New York Times*. Not good, and a heartbreaking response to the months of effort and talent and resources that we know went into the picture. Mind you, the film has its legions of fans, as any brisk trawl of the Internet will illustrate, and is shown quite regularly on television, most recently being on TCM in October 2008.

The impact left in the wake of *Alfred The Great* is still felt in parts of Galway and as recently as April 2008 we came across an advertisement in *The Tuam Herald*, explaining that there was *"an Al O'Dea table and six chairs, two carvers, in good condition, for sale"*, illustrating that the workmanship of O'Dea, Tom Dowd and all of their colleagues in Corrib Crafts was top drawer, as were the items they manufactured for Michael Stringer's sets. In his book from Currach Press in 2005, *The Story of Irish Film,* Arthur Flynn unwittingly hints at another possible reason for the dire outcome of the film. After explaining that the producers had to build their own studio close to the area in which they were filming (Kilchreest) because the Irish weather conditions were too unreliable to rely on Ardmore – founded in 1958 - Flynn moves on to Clive Donner, and explains that *Alfred The Great* was his first outdoor epic. Up to that, Donner had been admired for his taut, almost claustrophobic close-up shots in previous films, so the switch to vast panoramic outdoor vistas simply may not have suited his talents.

Numerous reasons have been proffered for the failure of the film, and the eventual disappointing outcome probably resulted from a combination of some or all of the explanations. In his foreword for this book Henry Comerford suggested that *"the concept was doomed from the beginning"* because the script fell between too many stools, all adding up to a *"fatal confusion of styles... at a time when tastes had changed".*

Other suggestions for its unsuccessful box office run include the fact that *Alfred The Great* was out of step with the times, being too bloodthirsty for the *'love and peace'* era that prevailed. David Hemmings, as suggested by Aidan Mooney (a retired teacher now but an extra then, as was John Fahy of Cummer), had insufficient gravitas to carry the weight of such a lumbering production. Prunella Ransome just disappears into the picture. The length of the film is an interminable 122 minutes, which is tricky enough when a movie is

David Hemmings about to knife an enemy viking from 'ATG"

VIKING SUMMER

spectacularly entertaining but tedious in the extreme when at least half of the production lags. The dialogue, too, was very old-fashioned and hard on the ears at a time when the kids were using a brand new lingua franca – *'cool', 'groovy', right on, man'* - that reached its apex a year later at Woodstock, and when the musical, *Hair*, was released.

Is it fair to question whether the producer, Bernard Smith, kept a tight enough grip on proceedings, and could it be that Clive Donner allowed himself to be distracted by lighting and other requirements on the film, to the detriment of his directorial responsibilities? Both suggestions were made to us.

Numerous observers have said that the editing of the picture made it drag even more, causing the whole thing to bog down in a swamp of treacle. The film, irony of ironies, was heaving with absolute authenticity at every level but that single minded, well-meaning quest for ninth-century perfection may have over-egged the pudding. Each distinct part looked fabulous but it didn't knit together into an enjoyable whole that had a beating heart with a distinctive narrative moving through a discernible beginning, middle and end. Too much time, effort and resources were wasted on minutiae and über-precision, time that may have been better spent on lubricating the script and injecting some pace, fun and impact into the production. The battle scenes (magnificent and all as they were) have been criticised for being both over-choreographed and for lacking rigid militaristic discipline, an impossible contradiction.

Fault lines may be found too in the fact that not enough trained stuntsmen were utilised in battle scenes, and the number of trained horses capable of 'acting' in those scenes were in insufficient supply. The movie was neither a satisfactory knuckle-dusting romp, nor was it a convincing evocation of a tortured internal monologue within Alfred. Really, vast swathes of it were collywobbles, and there's no other word for it. From the get-go, when MGM arrived in Ireland, expecting grey drizzly-grizzly weather, it was downhill from there on. That was the initial concept and it was blown out of the water from day one. They didn't want Hemmings to look 'pretty' even though it was his alluring persona in *Blow-Up* that actually got him the role, and yet he looked like the fifth Beatle in every single scene. Way too groovy for words, instead of the down-and-dirty appearance that had been planned. Finally, and most importantly of all, it's entirely possible that Lady Luck simply deserted the movie. *Casablanca* was made on a shoestring and it was never imagined that it would turn into such an iconic picture, but they got the 'rub of the green', it all fell together and the rest is history. It happens and as we learned, the film industry operates on the basis of one success to nine flops, the one hit picking up the financial slack of the nine.

The movie world trundles along, no matter that a few like *Alfred The Great* fall by the wayside and we've already learned that a large feature film, *Blood, Sweat and Tears* is to be filmed in Galway in 2008. The multimillion dollar *Mary, Queen of Scots* has got the go-ahead too and only time will tell whether they'll be 'the one' or be part of 'the nine'. Had *Alfred The Great* done the business, plans were well afoot to piggy-back an indigenous Irish movie industry (based at the purpose-built 12,000 square foot MGM studio complex in Kilchreest) on the back of that success. Ardmore had been up and running for ten years at this point but the Galway location was nicely positioned to make the most of its proximity to Shannon airport and its quick London turn-around time. Heaven and earth would have been moved to get the show on the road, had *Alfred* only made the cut. One man who was aware of discussions to encourage and establish a film industry at Kilchreest was Robert Molloy, who was Mayor of Galway during the making of *Alfred The Great* and met Hemmings in connection with the proposals in that mayoral capacity.

Mr. Molloy recalled being asked by David Hemmings to arrange a meeting with the relevant Minister involved with film making at the time, and that happened to be Patrick Hillery, a man who went on to serve two terms as President of Ireland and who passed away in early 2008. *"Paddy Hillery came down to Kilchreest where they were filming and Hemmings was on set - I remember Paddy had to wait about twenty minutes or so. It was out in the middle of a wilderness and they had a big fan there, with a fellow with a hose standing behind it making the rain and we had to struggle through it. Now that I think of it, I don't think I remember seeing that particular scene in the actual film,"* explained Mr. Molloy.

The making of the movie was a big deal in Galway city, much as we might have been led to think that it was a Castlehackett or Kilchreest 'country' project, and Molloy recalls that his brother Michael, a law student, was in it as was his future sister-in-law Martina, plus half the town. Every taxi driver and student seemed to have something to do with it too, he smiled, and that's why there was such huge disappointment when they eventually saw the finished product in the Odeon cinema in London's Leicester Square.

He doesn't know what transpired during the meeting between Hemmings and Patrick Hillery but Bobby Molloy was aware that there were great expectations of the film. *"People's past*

VIKING SUMMER

experience of films made in the west of Ireland was of The Quiet Man," he explained, *"so when they heard that another big production was being made here, with Lord Killanin involved again, they thought they were going to have another hit on their hands."* He surmised that the meeting may have been an attempt to help justify building such a gigantic studio complex in the middle of nowhere for just one film, and that might have been why Hemmings was trying to involve the Irish government in nurturing a movie industry there. It all came to nothing in the end but the pity was that Hemmings was at the peak of his career and had a big enough reputation at the time to carry such an undertaking and encourage other film companies to base their productions in Galway.

Mr. Molloy is not at all sure that the failure of *Alfred The Great* was directly responsible for the studio's failure to expand *"but surely it must have had some bearing on it. I was a recently elected TD (1965) and mayor (1968), so I didn't know how far plans had actually progressed but it's obvious that if the film had been a success, Hemmings would have gained huge kudos and his reputation would have soared with it."*

He was pleased to note that Hemmings came good again in later years and explained that he had known Al O'Dea of Corrib Crafts very well from swimming. That's a thread that runs though this story, via Christy Dooley, Lord Killanin being the IOC President at the time of the 1972 Olympics and Molloy being at those same games as the guest of the German government in his capacity as Minister of Sport. Robert Molloy recalled the huge assistance he received in the early 1960s from Lord Killanin when he and Christy Dooley and others were trying to get backing for the first indoor pool to be built in Galway. It was built eventually and was called after a famous Galwegian and swimming instructor, Jimmy Cranny, a man who actually taught my own mother to swim. Bobby Molloy recalled that he and John Huston, the film producer, and Dooley were in the middle of a meeting in the Imperial Hotel on Eyre Square concerning that swimming pool when they received the news that John F. Kennedy had been assassinated.

Robert Molloy was absolutely adamant that it was through the Killanin connection that *Alfred The Great* was brought to Galway – *"there's no doubt in the world about that"* – and he had great praise for David Hemmings and the work he put into the Mayoral concert that was held in the Rosary Hall, to raise funds for Biafra. The fact that a conman skipped off with the proceeds from the event didn't detract from the effort that went into its preparation, he said, adding that *"we know who he was and it isn't the first time he pulled*

Paddy and Ann Stewart of Roxburgh, Kilcreest, with their grandchild Kathryn. Lord Killanin wrote to them on MGM letterhead on 17th of October 1967 in his capacity as Production Associate, explaining that he was involved in the forthcoming production of Alfred the Great, *"which he hoped to film in Galway."* The letter went on to say *"one of the facilities we are looking for is an area in which to erect a temporary complex which would include facilities for shooting in bad weather."* Eventually a 24,000 sq ft concrete base was poured, 12,000 sq ft of which was covered for filming numerous interior scenes

Sean Stewart, Roxburgh, with his niece and god daughter Kathryn. Sean lent us his copies of the original planning permission for the MGM studio on the family farm

Sean Stewart, with his niece Maura (Molly) Stewart

a stunt like that." He has strong memories, too, of the mime artistry of Julian Chagrin from that show and was hugely appreciative of the voluntary efforts of all involved ."*When they were filming* Alfred The Great *I didn't have much to do with it, apart from being invited out to the set as a courtesy call,"* Mr. Molloy said. *"MGM was very welcome because of all of the employment they offered, even on a short-term basis, and we were all hoping it would be a success. But the cinema in London was practically empty when we were there. The word had got back to Galway that it was no good and it got very bad reviews at the time. I was disappointed at the failure to recognise as many people as I expected to in it and the film itself didn't seem to make a lot of sense, either."*

VIKING SUMMER

CAST

Alfred	David Hemmings
Guthrum	Michael York
Aelhswith	Prunella Ransome
Asher	Colin Blakely
Aethelstan	Julian Glover
Rober	Ian McKellen
Ethelred	Alan Dobie
Buhrud	Peter Vaughan
Ivar	Julian Chagrin
Wulfstan	Barry Jackson
Freda	Vivien Merchant
Cerdic	Christopher Timothy
Cuthbert	John Rees
Edwin	Andrew Bradford
Offa	Michael Billington
Bishop	Ralph Nossek
Olaf	David Glaisyer
Brother Thomas	Eric Brooks
Hadric	Keith Buckley
Sigurd	Trevor Jones
Eafa	Peter Blythe

Produced by Bernard Smith. Directed by Clive Donner. Screenplay by Ken Taylor and James R. Webb. Story by James R. Webb. From the novel by Eleanor Shipley Duckett. Director of Photography: Alex Thomson, B.S.C. Panavision and Metrocolor. Music Composed and Conducted by Raymond Leppard. Production Designer: Michael Stringer. Costume Designer: Jocelyn Rickards. Production Associate: Michael Killanin. In Charge of Production: Roy Parkinson. Second Unit Director: Brian Cummins. Art Director: Ernest Archer. Editor: Fergus McDonell. Sound Recordist: Cyril Swern. Assistant Director: Peter Price. Camera Operator: Tony Spratling. Continuity: Josephine Knowles. Casting Director: John Merrick. Make-Up: Tom Smith. Hairdresser: Alice Holmes. Sound Editor: Allan Sones. Battlemaster: Paul Stader. Special Effects: Robert A. MacDonad'd. A Bernard Smith-James R. Webb Production. Presented by Metro-Goldwyn-Mayer.

SUMMER SNOWBURN

In the first weeks of summer shooting, an unforeseen hazard for the MGM crew filming "Alfred the Great" on location in Galway, Ireland, proved to be — "snowburn." To recreate a snow-bound medieval village for the epic 9th century drama, starring David Hemmings, director Clive Donner ordered 60 tons of crushed marble to be spread on the five-acre set. The effect was completely convincing but the mid-day sun threw up a fierce glare from which there was no relief. Result—more than half the crew of "Alfred the Great" had to be treated for cases of mild to acute sunburn!

HEMMINGS SAID HE'D GIVE EYE TEETH TO PORTRAY "ALFRED" (AND HE DID!)

David Hemmings drew a blood-spattered hand wearily across his forehead, gritted his teeth, lifted a fearsome-looking sword high overhead and charged into the fray, where he sweated, strained, swung the sword, blocked blows, parried thrusts and proceeded to do no good whatsoever to the fighting image of the feared Viking invaders.

The scene in MGM's "Alfred the Great" was a re-creation of the battle of White Horse Hill (circa 871 A.D.), where the Saxon forces under Alfred put the Danish Viking invaders to flight and spared all Wessex and England to fight another day. For the film the battle took place on a hillside in County Galway, Ireland, which rang to the unfamiliar clatter of sword on shield, club on head and arrow in back as "Alfred the Great" committed to screen posterity the historic encounters between Saxon and Dane.

Withdrawing his sword from the "body" of a Dane, Hemmings, the blond, blue-eyed hero of "Blow-Up," rested his weary bones on the damp Irish turf.

"Well, if this doesn't finally erase my photographer image, nothing will," he said. "It's quite extraordinary how that 'Blow-Up' image has stuck. Actually, I'm not at all like that photographer."

To see Hemmings starring as England's legendary 9th century warrior king is to understand that a new aspect of this talented young actor will emerge on the screen. That of a noble, democratic and devout young king who was also a feared warrior. It is a prospect that pleases Hemmings.

"A visitor to the set asked me how I felt about accepting this role," said Hemmings. "What could I possibly answer? It's the most important role I've taken on to date, one which any actor would have given his eye teeth for. Come to think of it," he reflected, referring to an off-set accident that cost him two teeth, "that's exactly what I did!"

Hemmings insisted on fighting all his own battles with sword, lance and dagger without the help of professional stuntmen.

Commented director Clive Donner, "When David gets a sword in his hand he is remarkably proficient. He is also an excellent horseman. He has great style and dash." Hollywood stuntman Paul Stader added to the commendation. "He is the most coordinated actor I've ever worked with," he stated. No small praise from a man who dived from the hanging lianas in all Johnny Weissmuller's "Tarzan" adventures and laid about him with swords for Errol Flynn's derring-do movies. Hemmings eased himself off the ground and prepared once more to tackle his Viking opponents.

"I think you could say this has been a strenuous role," he said, wryly. "But I've enjoyed it so much that I wouldn't mind accepting another of this genre. But then, I suppose if I did, it would take me years to escape from the 'physical' rut.

"You can't win, can you?" he concluded, plunging back into the milling bodies with a blood-curdling yell."

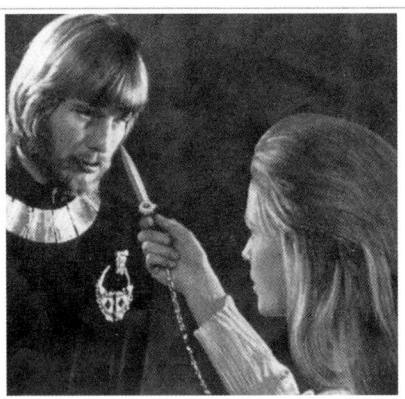

Aelhswith (Prunella Ransome), King Alfred's wife, held as a hostage by Guthrum (Michael York), leader of the Danish Vikings, threatens him with a dagger when he tries to force his attentions on her. The scene is from "Alfred the Great," MGM's epic drama of England's first hero-king, with Alfred Hemmings in the title role. Depicting some of the most spectacular battles ever shown on the screen, the massive Bernard Smith-James R. Webb production was filmed in its entirety on locations in Ireland in Panavision and Metrocolor under the direction of Clive Donner.

Promotional Cast Information
This publicity extract lists all of the cast in MGM's *Alfred The Great* and describes the sunburn suffered by actors when the hot summer sun bounced off the white Connemara marble used to form a blanket of snow on location at the Kilchreest studio

As we wrapped up this merry saga Jim Norton was beginning to receive sustained plaudits for his role in *The Boy In The Striped Pyjamas*, proof, as if more were needed, that the acting quality was there in *Alfred The Great* all along, but obviously wasn't enough to tip the scales in the right direction.

David Lean himself explained in Michael Tanner's fantastic book, *Troubled Epic*, that once he set his mind on a film project, he liked to get on with it as quickly as possible, moving through the process of script preparation as briskly as possible, *"because I hate it really! I'm not a word man, I like pictures."* As far as Lean was concerned, the moments you remember in movies are often not dialogue at all, rather they consist of images, in combination with soaring evocative music. That's what moves an audience. In *Alfred's* case, there are some majestic shots and images that will certainly stand the test of time, even if the less

This grainy black and white photo with two little girls, Noleen and Maura Stewart, in the foreground, was taken in 1968 from the Stewart's house, looking towards the newly built MGM studio complex. Imediately behind the studio, right across the road, is Kilcreest Castle. There is scaffolding around it, which MGM crew used to climb up to 'square-off' the crumbling battlements at the top of the castle

said about the dialogue, the better. Elements of the uplifting panoramic shots that litter both Lean's *Dr. Zhivago* and *Ryan's Daughter* seeped into the fabric of *Alfred The Great*, infused circuitously via Donner's early years spent learning his craft at the feet of Lean, and they carry their own cinematic rapture. In all fairness, we must credit Clive Donner with that achievement.

The entrance of the MGM studio complex, 2008

Kilcreest Castle, with its crumbling battlements at the top, 2008

VIKING SUMMER

In another reference to *Ryan's Daughter,* Tanner's book explains that the planners knew full well that the main danger of the movie *"lay in the possibility of the film falling calamitously between two stools; too glossy for a simple love story, too superficial for authoritative history"* – and that quandary certainly rings a few bells with regard to poor old *Alfred The Great.*

It's a tricky balance to get right, often impossible, with so many imponderables pushing and pulling the director in so many different directions, but Lean might have put his finger on the nub of the business of movie-making when he explained that *"the most important thing of all is to find a story that you can fall in love with... and I've got to know the script, the intention of it and the characters in it better than anybody else."* Could that have been the problem with Alfred – nobody loved it quite enough? Certainly Smith and Donner took it on as a project that they felt would be a successful picture at the box office, bolstered by Hemmings' public persona at the time, but one never gets the impression while watching it that it had a beating heart and soul like a daft ould movie such as *The Quiet Man*. Of course they're radically different pictures and can't be compared at any level, but it's an interesting thought. *Alfred The Great* was actually more authentic and true to its time than the begorrah nonsense of the the Wayne/O'Hara masterpiece, but it didn't capture the heart or the imagination of the audience. It was a sturdy, worthy film made up of zillions of different pieces that had all been individually honed to perfection, but the eventual whole never exceeded its constituent parts.

It was fascinating to learn that the translation from Irish of the name, Castle Hackett, is actually 'a thicket' and would it be too fanciful to suggest that Clive Donner might have lost his way in the wooded, tree-lined slopes of Knockma, led astray in the thickets by the hosts of ghosts and fairies and 'little people' who supposedly make the hill their home?

Professor Kevin Rockett, Head of the Film School in Trinity College in Dublin, told us that *Alfred The Great* isn't an Irish film, as such, and has never appeared in his many writings and research on Irish film because *"it is a film which I would categorise as using Ireland as 'another location'."* In that context *Alfred* is neither fish nor fowl, and can't benefit from its Irish links in the same hilariously blatant manner as Micheleen Óg, Sean Thornton and Mary Kate Danaher in John Ford's rousing *The Quiet Man.*

We visited Cong and Ashford Castle on Father's Day 2008, when the June sun was shining, and the place was hopping with tourists, the vast majority of whom were bounding in and out of gift shops, buying their Quiet Man tee-shirts, clasping their Quiet Man calendars to their breasts and popping their Quiet Man postcards into the nearby mail box.

When we see a tourism flurry like that at Castlehackett, Kilchreest, Killinure and Roscahill, we will know that the making of *Alfred The Great* on location in County Galway in the summer of 1968 has left a tangible legacy. For the moment, like the dog who walked on his hind legs, the remarkable thing about MGM's *Alfred The Great* was not the fact that it might have been done poorly, but that it was ever done at all.

THE END

BIBLIOGRAPHY

1. Hughes, Michael J., *Caherlistrane GAA and 150 Years of Parish Life* (1990, Printed by *The Tuam Herald*)

2. Hughes, Michael J., *History and Folklore of the Barony of Clare* {Co. Galway}, (1997, Printed by *The Connacht Tribune*)

3. Best, George, *Blessed, The Autobiography* with co-author Roy Collins (2001, Ebury Press)

4. Burt, Angela, *Quick Solutions to Common Errors in English* (2004, How To Books Ltd, Oxford)

5. Harbison, Peter, *A Thousand Years of Church Heritage in East Galway* (2005, Ashfield Press)

6. Semple, Maurice, *By The Corribside* (1984, Published by the author)

7. Kummer, Ditty, *Ireland Explored, An Illustrated Travel Guide* (1986, Brandon)

8. Smiley, Jane, *Ten Days in the Hills* (2007, Alfred A Knopf)

9. Smith, Bernard, *A World Remembered*

10. O'Brien, Pat, *A Book of Genesis* (1988, Salmon)

11. Lynch, Donal, *The Kirwans of Castlehackett* (2007, Four Courts Press)

12. Rikards, *Jocelyn, Banquet*

13. Murphy, J.J., *Guide to The Quiet Man*

14. McNee, Gerry, *In The Footsteps of The Quiet Man* (1990, Mainstream)

15. Hemmings, *David, Blow-Up and Other Exaggerations* (2004)

16. York, Michael, *Travelling Player* (2001)

17. Tanner, Michael, *Troubled Epic* (2007)

18. Cunningham, Dr. John, *A Town Tormented by the Sea*

19. Cavander, Kenneth, *Behind The Scenes*

20. Flynn, Arthur, *Cinema in Ireland* (2005, Currach Press)

ABOUT THE AUTHOR

Mary J. Murphy has been a journalist and broadcaster for twenty years and is a past pupil of both Ballinruane National School and Holy Rosary College, Mountbellew. Following her B.A. degree in English Literature from University College Galway she did the Postgraduate Journalism programme in DCU's (then NIHE) Department of Communications, under Professor John Horgan, specialising in radio, and went on to co-found the NEWS-CELLAR press agency with journalism colleagues.

She has worked from abroad (Iceland, Nashville and London), has served as Ireland correspondent for *The Universe (UK)*, has written for *The New Zealand Star* and has been published widely in publications that include *The Irish Times, The Sunday Tribune, The Evening Herald, The Irish Independent* and *The Irish Press*. In Dublin she produced and presented her own radio show and has made numerous contributions to RTE Radio 1, Galway Bay FM, Clare FM and Mid-West Radio over the years. Mary was a press officer for the Galway Arts Festival, taught English briefly following a postgraduate TEFL Certificate in UCG, has written documentary scripts and has carried out in-depth research and historical projects. She writes a weekly music column for *The Connacht Tribune* and is currently working on her next book. With her husband and three children, she lives at the south-western foothills of Knockma.

(Copies of this book are available from morma@eircom.net and from 086 27 67 730)

This book celebrates the memory and the too-short life
of our tiny baby son, Michael Andrew Glynn.
(RIP July 2006)